OTHER WAYS TO WIN

A COMPETITIVE CYCLIST'S REFLECTIONS ON SUCCESS

LEE CRAIGIE

Vertebrate Publishing, Sheffield
www.adventurebooks.com

OTHER WAYS TO WIN

Lee Craigie

First published in 2023 by Vertebrate Publishing.

VERTEBRATE PUBLISHING, Omega Court, 352 Cemetery Road, Sheffield S11 8FT, United Kingdom. *www.adventurebooks.com*

Front cover: The author riding in Fisherfield, Scotland. Photo: Maciek Tomiczek.

Illustration on page ix by Emily Crookshank.

This book is a work of non-fiction based on the life of Lee Craigie. The author has stated to the publishers that, except in such minor respects not affecting the substantial accuracy of the work, the contents of the book are true. Some names and incidental details have been changed to protect the privacy of contributors.

A CIP catalogue record for this book is available from the British Library.

ISBN: 978-1-83981-206-4 (Paperback)

ISBN: 978-1-83981-207-1 (Ebook)

ISBN: 978-1-83981-208-8 (Audiobook)

10 9 8 7 6 5 4 3 2 1

Edited by Moira Hunter, cover design by Jane Beagley.

Vertebrate Publishing is committed to printing on paper from sustainable sources.

Printed and bound in Great Britain by Clays Ltd, Elcograf S.p.A.

CONTENTS

To my funny, kind, supportive family. Because my stories are your stories.

To Alice, for all our future stories.

I was standing on a cliff edge in the semi-darkness. Out of my back had sprouted two gigantic, grotesque wings that flexed, creaked and groaned, spreading out so large they obscured my entire naked frame. These magnificent, malevolent appendages of feather and muscle were so huge and powerful that their raw feral beauty frightened her even in her dream.

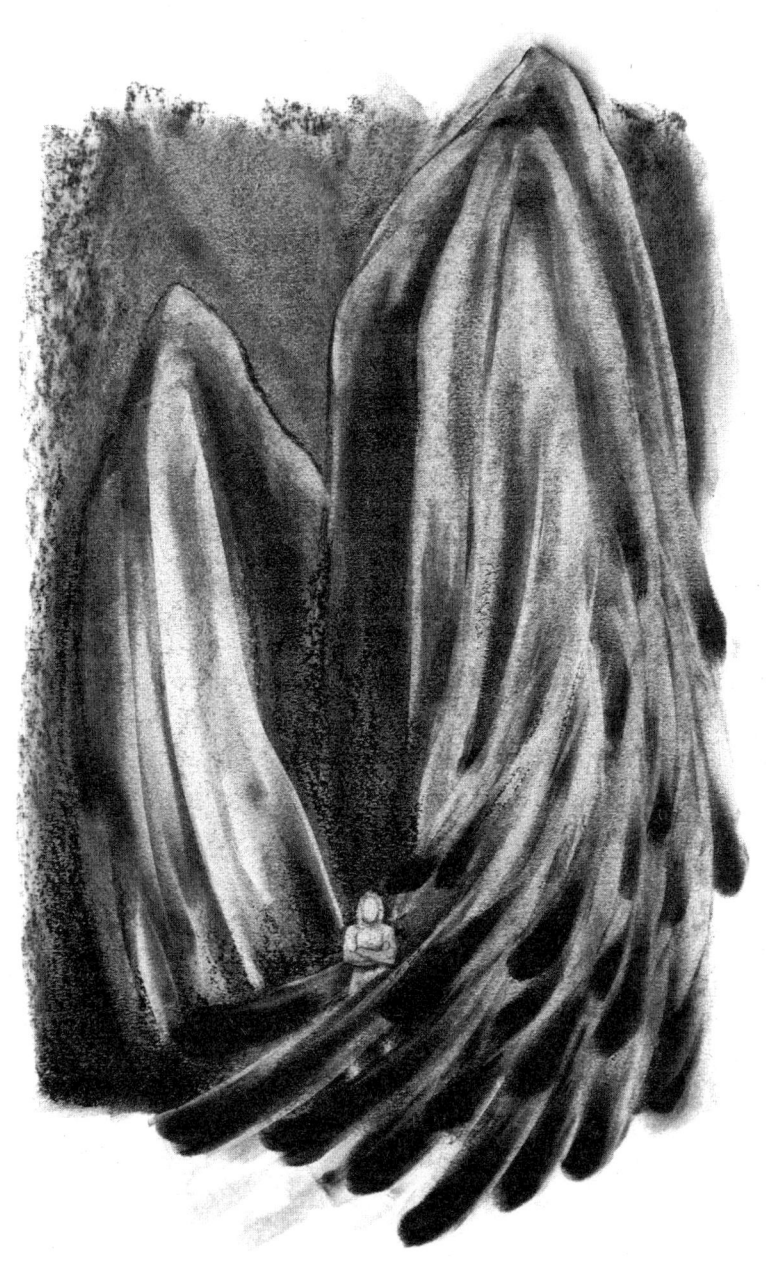

PREFACE

I'm sitting at a worn wooden table in front of a glass wall that so far this morning has shown me only my own reflection. Out of the corner of my eye, the wood-burning stove flickers orange and gathers strength with a throaty purr, the smell of woodsmoke from its initial refusal to light still lingering about the tiny space. My porridge sits in a cast-iron pan on the stove top. It is 6.40 a.m. It will be a while yet before my breakfast is ready to eat. I'll know when that time has come because the weak winter sun will have risen enough to obscure my reflection in the glass and reveal the Isle of Rum instead. It won't be a shock when this happens. It's a gradual shift from the current introspection of my little wooden cabin to the drama of the outside world. Soon Rum's outrageous snow-dusted peaks will sit stoic and majestic on its watery foundations. By then the cabin will be roasting hot, but right now I am wrapped in a warm woollen blanket with a pot of coffee on the table next to me. The wind is up outside. Something metallic is clattering in the distance, but it's the whistling, whooshing noise that is stopping me from fully acknowledging my need to visit the composting toilet. It is only twenty metres away but I'm still sleepy and feeling vulnerable to the cold.

I'm at Sweeney's Bothy, a beautifully crafted tiny home of wood and corrugated iron perched below an amphitheatre of chossy crags on the Isle of Eigg. For years, writers, poets, artists and musicians have been coming here, choosing to replace the stimuli of phone reception and other humans with the more sensorially enhancing stimuli of the natural world. At Sweeney's I feel part of the landscape, which I suppose I am wherever I go, but it's easier to feel this in some places than in others.

In a world where it feels like we are growing too fast for our own skin and we seem unable to accept the changes we know will make our world healthier, happier and fairer, Eigg folds its arms and rocks back on its heels, whistling through its teeth at us. It seems to say, 'I told you so.'

Eigg sits nestled in the Sound of Sleat below Skye, sheltered from the Atlantic by the Outer Hebrides. It's a tiny island, only five miles by three but with a breathtaking diversity of landscape. In 1997 Eigg made history by becoming the first community-owned island (and only the second community-owned estate) in Scotland. Since then it has established its own renewable energy systems and built and managed essential community resources for the good of its residents and visitors. While I'm quite sure none of this was easy, it clearly wasn't impossible, and now Eigg is a living, breathing example of how sustainable communities might develop given enough autonomy.

Sweeney's Bothy on Eigg feels like a fitting place to come to finish a collection of stories that explore other ways to win.

My task was to write an autobiographical account for a publishing house whose strapline is 'Inspiring Adventure'. The thought of doing that initially made me feel a bit squeamish. I thought I might have some entertaining stories to tell that could even offer up a different perspective, but the idea of writing a chronological memoir of my life felt self-indulgent at best and megalomaniacal at worst. So, I wrote this book for myself in the same spirit as I hope each individual who picks it up interprets it, with their own bias and background.

Spoiler alert: there is no definitive way to win. My only hope is that these stories inspire some sort of personal reflection on what winning means for each of us, but also what it means to us as part of something much bigger and wilder and timeless.

The sky here has now separated itself from the earth and the sea is beginning to separate itself from the sky. All three are variations on the colour blue. The wind hasn't dropped one wee bit, but its soundtrack is now enhanced by the shadows of the whipping bare birch branches outside. Rum is revealed. Impossibly close and oppressively high. The room is warm and my porridge is ready. I'll leave you to your own reality now.

CHAPTER 1
BELIEVING & BEGINNING

I can't have been more than seven years old when I first felt it. My memories of the moment are all tilted and jumbled, and it's just possible they aren't even real memories at all but the wild imaginings of my younger self. It doesn't really matter. What is real is how I feel when I conjure up the image of that place even now.

I'm alone on a wide valley floor below a very, very big mountain. It's dusk and there's a dampness and a deep chill in the air. I'm still the right side of cold but only just. I have a vague awareness that safety and warmth and other people aren't far away, but despite my instincts tugging me towards those things, I don't go. Instead, I take a few steps in the opposite direction towards the terrifying outline of the unbelievable shape filling my horizon. I want to scratch the itch, to stretch the elastic, feel my excitement tip further towards fear. There is nothing between me and this formidable shape in the gloom, and I can feel the ominous scale of it, the sheer size and possessing gravitas of it. I'm shivering now and aware of a deep stirring low down in my abdomen. It's not the thing itself that's having this effect on me, it's my interaction with it. I'm imagining myself whisked to the top of it where I would feel completely lost and powerless in the throes of its wildness. I would be blind in the cloud cover and beaten by the wind and the rain. I'd be so cold and scared up there, completely unable to find safety and warmth. I both wanted it and it was the last thing in the world I wanted. I didn't understand what I was feeling then. I do now.

We all crave comfort and convenience. We live busy lives and time is precious, so we quite rightly try to make things as easy and efficient as possible, but in general most of us not living in poverty or in war zones shy away from discomfort and challenge more than we need to. When I think about why I crave travelling by bike in unfamiliar places or in unpredictable mountain environments it's certainly not because it's comfortable or convenient. It's the complete opposite. I find when I remove excessive choice, comfortable familiarity and easy routine then the chatter eases in my busy brain. When I have something challenging to push against then I'm forced back into my body and life becomes simple and, counter-intuitively, it becomes joyful again. Sometimes less really is more.

I grew up in a small town to the north of Glasgow, not far from the Campsie Fells and even less far from Lenzie Moss, a patch of mixed woodland and raised bog. In this diverse peatland ecosystem on the edge of one of Scotland's largest cities, life thrummed and bristled in sweet-smelling damp ground. Scraggly birch, willow, alder and rowan arranged themselves with as much dignity as could be mustered in the crumbling earth, while heathers and mosses clung to the peaty soil for dear life. Frogs and dragonflies made regular appearances in my young life and helped me form a rudimentary understanding of the seasons. Birdsong could deafen at certain times of the day and give an eight-year-old, completely immersed in a guddle of frogspawn, the same information an alarm on her wristwatch might. Exploring the Moss at night often revealed the glinting eyes and retreating tails of foxes or the white stripe of a badger, the excitement eradicating any feelings of cold, fear or hunger that may have existed moments before. When I ventured up the Moss, particularly in fading light or if the weather was bad, I would often feel alone, scared, wet, cold and tired, but I knew with the instincts of a child that feeling those things opened the door to feeling alive.

I loved every inch of Lenzie Moss. Over a period of years, I got to know every tree root, rock and peat hag in that one square mile, so that the place came to feel almost like a member of my own family.

Perhaps the biggest gift I was given as a child was the permission to explore the Moss alone. Back then I was much better at feeling content and happy in a small, familiar landscape. My autonomous world hadn't yet widened beyond that one square mile and, importantly, at eight years old I didn't know what I still didn't know. I had everything I needed and complete freedom from desire to travel further into unknown wilderness. I was aware other wild places existed, but they were exotic domains belonging to David Bellamy or David Attenborough, whose worlds were confined to a tiny box in the living room. There was no competition between them and my wild, physical world, wedged as it was between the train line to the city and a busy main road. The familiarity of the Moss, combined with the encouragement to explore it from parents whose protective instincts had thankfully been dulled by my older sister's fight for autonomy, offered unparalleled freedom to my creative imaginings.

I'm grateful that my older sister paved the way for me. Kim took the brunt of the natural anxiety that comes with having no clue what to do when you become a parent for the first time. My mum and dad made all their mistakes with Kim and so when I came along three years later, they could apply all they had learned to develop a balanced, serene, confident, perfect child this time around. This is what I tell Kim. She disagrees.

Three years is a dangerous gap between siblings. Kim and I were close enough in age to play together, but any protective, empathic instincts the older sibling might feel with a bigger age gap were very much missing. Kim often made me cry, but on one unforgettable occasion she tried to shut me up by shoving toilet paper in my mouth. When the terror at having my main airway blocked began registering in my bulging eyes, Kim pulled the paper out of my mouth with such vigour that two of my teeth came with it. There was a stunned silence as we both stared at the little white specks lodged in the pink tissue before the tears, this time accompanied by blood and pain, started again. At this stage most big sisters would accept defeat and allow a parent to be summoned. But not my sister.

Quick as lightning she picked up the teeth and manoeuvred in front of me so I could see the animation in her face.

'Lee. Listen. LISTEN. I've got a BRILLIANT idea!' In the time it took me to draw a snotty breath she explained that we had a unique, once-in-a-lifetime opportunity to prove the existence of the Tooth Fairy.

I would not tell my parents what had happened. Instead, we would change places at the dinner table that night so that neither of them would notice my gummy right side. At bedtime I would place the teeth under my pillow and await our supernatural visitation. My sister was clever and quick-witted, but she was not so clever and quick-witted as to realise she might buy herself even more time from being chastised by my parents if she put two 50p pieces under my pillow that night. Instead, the lack of coins the following morning broke my heart and caused me to troop downstairs wailing at the injustice of the entire situation. I felt I deserved some comfort and vindication from my mum. If there was justice, I would receive an explanation and an apology from this woman who, for years, had lied consistently about the existence of the Tooth Fairy and who knows what else. I would be given a cuddle for having suffered the trauma of the previous day so stoically and all alone. My sister would be summoned and punished for her bullying and manipulation. Instead, my mum said:

'That's not how it works, Lee. You have to tell me first so I can ring the Tooth Fairy and let her know our address.'

I shouldn't have been surprised. Kim had to get her clever quick-wittedness from somewhere.

My mother, Lesley, like my sister, trained as a PE teacher, but both have worked exclusively with children with special educational needs. Both Lesley and Kim could have gone to art school, but both chose PE college instead, a decision that niggles at them from time to time. This meant that our household was a competitively creative and liberal place to grow up. It was expected that our bodies would perform physically and that our minds would grow outside the narrow confines of the education system.

Lenzie was a traditional place made up of 2.4-children households. Often mums would stay at home while dads worked nine to five in offices or factories in Glasgow before returning home expecting mince and tatties on the table at 6 p.m. This didn't work for Lesley. She was a striking, confident, energetic woman who drove a green and white Citroën 2CV while wearing a German tank commander's outfit. She was, and still is, a staunch feminist and equalitarian who liked to rock the Lenzie boat at every opportunity. When I was a child this was a crippling embarrassment. Now I am incredibly grateful to her for teaching me never to unthinkingly accept things the way they are. The small-mindedness of this small town in the dreich south-west of Scotland might have severely restricted my developing imagination and stunted my ambition, but because I had a mum who smoked cigars and played international squash I was allowed to believe that anything was possible. Now in her seventies, Lesley continues to work as a dance movement therapist. She is a passionate advocate of the power of non-verbal communication for people with severe disabilities so that they might have some autonomy over the way they communicate in this black and white world. She continues to encourage me to think outside the box every day.

My dad is a handsome, funny, kind man who owned a knitwear factory in the east end of Glasgow and who returned from work every evening smelling of lanolin and engine oil. Ken was privately educated at Dollar Academy and believed that 'Margaret Thatcher was the best thing to ever happen to this country', so it's perhaps unsurprising that my parents separated when I was twelve years old. Lesley and Ken made an unlikely pair and in the end their differences began to erode their deep fondness for each other. They managed to save their friendship by calling it quits early, meaning that decades later they still have a friendship based on a shared sense of humour, lots of memories and two grown-up daughters.

Ken could light up a room just by ambling in with his easy, un-affected grace and his big grin. Nothing ruffled him and he never took anything too seriously. In retrospect this must have infuriated poor Lesley who was left to hold all the boundaries, feed us and make sure our clothes were on the right way round. If left in Ken's hands all weekend Kim and I might have eaten nothing but sardines and Chelsea buns and stayed up building dens in the woods until late. Being around him was easy and fun and, as a result, I was usually never more than a few feet away from him.

As adults I have been mistaken for my sister on countless occasions, and these days we make an unbeatable team in Pictionary because we know instinctively how the other's mind works, but our differences in personality have always been obvious. While Kim would shout and scream, I would be more likely to take myself off and sulk. In circumstances where she would get angry and give up on a task, I would grit my teeth and, with pale-faced determination, persevere until I had exhausted myself or overcome the challenge. Watching Kim from my low-down perspective taught me so much about the world before I got to the stage in my life where I had to step up to its challenges. I had the privilege of seeing the weight of the world's expectations on someone else's shoulders before it was my turn to bear them. It also meant I had three years to covet a set of yellow and blue roller boots, a green parka jacket and a handsome little red BMX bike with silver graphics. I'm sure there were more hand-me-downs than that during my childhood, but these were the ones I remember most vividly and, to be completely honest, as soon as I inherited that bike, the longed-for roller boots and jacket paled into insignificance.

I called the bike Kit. I was seven and at a stage in my life when I would happily spend every waking hour embodying the character Michael Knight from the popular 1980s programme *Knight Rider*. Kit was Michael's intelligent talking car that could drive itself and was always saving Michael from tricky situations. Michael and Kit were a crime-solving duo and the most exciting partnership I could imagine. I spent all of my spare time riding around the neighbourhood or up to the edge of the Moss on my two-wheeled Kit, pretending I was solving crimes and saving people. I would spend hours getting better and better at pulling skids, popping off kerbs, riding out of the saddle and balancing stationary. Kit and I performed the same movements over and over again, but it never felt as though I was practising skills in the way I had to in gym class or on tennis courts.

These were the perfect learning conditions for me. No one watching, lots of space, unlimited time and no targets or milestones to reach. I would get so engrossed in the moment under these conditions that hours would disappear. By instinctively responding to the resistance the pedals and handlebars offered my hands and feet, I experienced a deep thrill from the incremental skill gain that caused me to feel more and more in control of my own physicality.

I've had many bikes since Kit and I've felt an affinity with lots of them, but I can still conjure up the particular feeling of that hard little saddle and the worn plastic handlebar grips, and how my small frame fitted the space between them perfectly. I can still remember the effortlessness of standing up to cant the little bike from side to side by pulling with one arm and pushing with the opposite leg, and in doing so propel the whole squiggling, writhing mass of metal and limbs forwards at a surprising speed.

Bike riding back then opened a door between my brain and body but also further fuelled my already firing imagination. Becoming more physically and emotionally confident as a result of incessant bike handling had allowed me my first glimpses of real, grown-up euphoria. The feelings I was getting from having mastered the complex skill of riding a bike were nothing short of magical. Young Michael Knight was obsessed with the feeling of moving unencumbered and she was already craving the endorphins this released when she found herself confined inside.

I vividly remember waking early one morning having dreamt that Kit and I could fly. I got out of bed and put on the same jumper and green tracksuit trousers that I wore every day of my young life, then quietly opened the heavy front door just enough to squeeze outside. The cold of the morning filled my nose making my eyes water. By the time I had dragged Kit out of the garage and ridden the 500 metres to the edge of the Moss, my core temperature had ramped considerably while the cold had robbed my hands and chin of their ability to move normally. I stood astride the bike, my Green Flash trainers sinking into the muddy, overgrown football pitch that led into the trees, and closed my eyes. I breathed deeply, allowing my dream to surface again until it buzzed and crackled over my scalp, a tangible energy that I just knew, with a seven-year-old's certainty, I could turn into flight. I started riding, pumping my legs faster and faster, utterly convinced that at any moment my tyres would leave the ground and I would soar over the trees like a bird of prey. When I was at maximum velocity I pulled up on my bars with every sinew of muscle not pumping the pedals. When it didn't happen I was pretty surprised, but I wasn't disappointed. I knew I *could* fly. I just had in my dream. This feeling of something magical and powerful that I didn't quite understand, but that I knew existed in me, is probably felt by the vast majority of young people lucky enough to grow up free from harm and with encouragement to be curious. That morning, although my bike and I had remained firmly on the frosty ground, I had just experienced magic. My imagination had allowed me to sidestep rational limitations. My memory of that morning is tinged with what I've come to call 'adultrospect': the remembering of childhood wonder with cynicism and slight scorn but also with envy. We grow up and forget how able we once were. There is real wisdom in the naivety of children. I don't think the word 'naivety' should be interchangeable with the word ignorance. These wonders still wait for us in the corners of our minds if we can quieten the intellectualising, fearful, disappointed adult in all of us. Sometimes all it takes is closing your eyes and flapping your arms a bit.

The first inklings that the limits to my ability might be simply the fabrications of other people's minds came to me in the shape of a lawn mower, one of those old petrol ones that weighs a ton and reeks of engine oil and sour, fermenting grass. It was late summer so the evening was still light and warm. My family had eaten dinner and the gentle rumblings of bedtime were just beginning to emanate in my direction. As the youngest member of any family knows, this is always the time to leap into action. There are a great many things a seven-year-old can do at this stage in an evening to divert the bedtime bulldozer. Beginning conversations on educational topics with parents can be highly effective but depends on the adults' willingness to engage. Making yourself tiny and inconspicuous can be useful if you sense the adult is weary and lacking in resolve. But on balance I found that helping with chores was by far the most consistently effective way to stall the inevitability of bedtime. On this particular evening my dad was outside with the lawn mower on the little square of grass that made up the majority of our back garden. He was pulling violently on the starting cord of the old mower, his whole body jerking powerfully up and away from the machine again and again while the engine hacked and whined but stubbornly refused to ignite. I made my way outside and stood quietly at a distance from him trying to gauge the mood. If he was getting frustrated then it might be more prudent to return indoors and hide behind the sofa (a tried and tested technique for avoiding bedtime), thus avoiding any direct order to go to bed.

Clouds had begun to bruise the dusky sky and despite the lawn mower's protestations trying to drown it out, birdsong was rising to fever pitch. I felt full of energy. My body was still tingling with the exertions of an afternoon spent playing football in the sun and the thought of having to lie down indoors filled me with something approaching horror. I resolved then and there to give it my best shot. I did not want to be inside on a night that felt so full of potential, even safely behind the sofa. I was willing to risk rejection in an effort to establish my usefulness in this outside task.

'Dad. Can I have a go?'

My dad's initial reaction didn't fill me with hope. 'You won't be able to start it if I can't, love.'

'Can I just have a go? Please.'

Result. A despondent and indulgent smile followed by his retreat to the kitchen had bought me a few minutes at least. I picked up the cord and tried to pull it back in the way he had done, but my lack of strength and conviction meant the motor caught the cord immediately and pulled the plastic handle from my grip. It hurt a bit and my resolve weakened. I tried again and again, and each time I understood a little more what was required of the motion to achieve the desired result. My technique evolved until I was wrapping both hands around the plastic handle and using one foot to brace the machine. I pulled hard and this time I heard the motor catch briefly before dying again. A sliver of excitement pierced me low in my abdomen. I turned quickly to see if anyone was watching. I was alone. The sun had sunk considerably lower in the sky since my first attempt and a chill had begun to creep into the air around me. It was now dusk and I was alone in the garden operating important adult machinery. I should definitely be in bed by now. Such liberty at this time of night felt illicit and intoxicating. I tried again. And again. And again until the muscles in my shoulder and forearm felt that they might burst out of my skin. I felt a bit sick from the struggle but nowhere near the end of my resolve to get the mower started. I stopped and crouched next to it, one knee pressing into the long, soft grass. I visualised myself standing up, bracing the metal bulk of the mower with one foot, seizing the cord and pulling it hard with both hands, right up behind my ear. A surge of adrenaline coursed through me and I knew for absolute certainty that on my next attempt the engine was going to start. When it did, and it sent out its rasping cry for the whole neighbourhood to hear, I wasn't surprised but I was delighted and I turned around to find all three members of my immediate family standing slack-jawed at the kitchen window.

This was the start of a very important series of realisations for me. That even when there is no evidence to suggest a thing is possible, it might be so. That even when all the people you trust in the world are giving you their version of your reality in a way that dampens your spirit and undermines your fragile self-confidence, the remarkable can still happen. That in trying something using creativity and child-like imaginings, outcomes can be generated that no one, not even the wisest of adults, could have predicted or can explain. That we are all capable of so much more than we think we are, and that we should never let anyone put a limit on that ambition and squash our curiosity. That even the heroes of gripping lawn mower resurrection stories can be told to go to bed.

As I grew older, things began to feel less and less simple. My wild imagination and absorption in the natural world gave way to bouts of feeling really low and devoid of any motivation to be outside and active. It came at the same time as my body began changing into a woman's body and I wasn't sure I liked it any more. My gender had not really featured in my sense of self before now and with puberty came the shock of societal expectation. The exciting realisation that there was a huge world out there was dampened by these unwelcome biological advances into adulthood and the fact that despite them I still wasn't old enough to explore it yet. For the next million years my days were going to be spent sitting still in hot classrooms learning how little I knew. I spent vast amounts of time imagining my future (never a recipe for contentedness) and wished for time to pass more quickly so that I might get out there and start discovering who I was rather than what society and biology expected me to be.

CHAPTER 2
THE CAMPSIE FELLS

My sister and I both looked like wee boys as kids. When my mum took Kim to meet her first teacher in the days leading up to her starting primary school, five-year-old Kim boldly introduced herself as Ross and, pointing to the buggy my mum was pushing, me as her brother Nigel. Back in the 1980s when gender was less of a fluid concept than it is now, our tomboy status caused a few raised eyebrows, but our mum in particular shrugged it off on our behalf. As we emerged into adulthood, societal pressure intensified and we felt forced to choose which side of the gender divide we were on. Kim emerged from her world of tracksuit bottoms and spiked hair into an attractive, popular teenage girl, who neatly fitted the female mould, but when it was my turn, I found it harder to let go of the Nigel in me.

In the first few weeks of my first year of secondary school, while others scrabbled frantically to make allies in the melting pot of feeder primary schools, I stood aloof and distant, ostracising myself from them all. Practising aloof indifference seemed less frightening than risking outright rejection. It seemed that in order to fit in I had to care about things I did not. It seemed I had to follow an unspoken code that meant ignoring some girls and fawning over others. Most alarmingly, though, it seemed I was expected to grow my hair and wear make-up. The thought of this made me feel physically sick. It wasn't that I was being stubborn in my refusal to conform to looking more stereotypically female, it was because I physically couldn't stomach the idea of it.

I kept my hair cropped short and witnessed in silent dismay the changes my disloyal body was going through without my permission. Widening hips and budding breasts left me feeling confused and uncoordinated, and any confidence and sense of self that had built up over the years from being fluid and supple on and off my bike quickly ebbed away.

I wished I could have felt okay about growing my hair and wearing different clothes, but to do so was unthinkable then. It would have felt easier removing my own eyes. No one understood this and I couldn't articulate it, so instead I kept my head down and wished away time. Every day I suffered some level of verbal bullying, mostly from the boys in my year, and gradually I built up a wall around my tender adolescent seed of a self. I developed a lofty grace and used my sense of humour to deflect attention away from what I looked like. These survival tactics sometimes worked and earned me a reputation for not caring what teachers thought of me, when deep down I was cripplingly insecure and desperate to be anywhere other than the school building.

Without a circle of friends around me at school, I walked the corridors of Lenzie Academy like a wounded animal estranged from the security of the rest of the pack and completely exposed to attack from predators. My peers couldn't accept my lack of femininity and at the same time keep a grasp on their fragile sense of the world. Not much feels certain in adolescence. The desperation to conform and to have others do the same is understandable, even forgivable when you consider how much hormonal turmoil young adults are in.

Conforming to social norms makes so much sense. If your face fits with the majority of other faces, then the heat of any potential conflict gets dissipated amongst many. The struggles and challenges that exist every minute of the day for those who don't fit in cause life to simmer at a constantly higher temperature. Living in a state of constant fear and always on high alert is at best exhausting and isolating, and at worst absolutely terrifying.

I knew even then that the 'othering' of people who don't fit neatly into the boxes we create to keep our own world view in order is the ultimate ugliness of humans and that by giving into that I would not only lose my sense of self but my self-respect too.

My time at secondary school was very difficult, but there was nothing that could have prepared me better for the unconventional life I would lead later on. It's easier to go against the flow if you never fitted in to begin with. When you don't have anything to lose, then taking risks isn't so scary.

I regret skipping French class now. Of all the learning from my school days that might have come in useful to me as an adult, speaking French and ceilidh dancing would have proved the most relevant. Yet it was my rejection of French class that in a convoluted way allowed me to discover what I might be capable of achieving on a mountain bike.

The French classroom was always a stuffy post-lunchtime fug of woollen blazers that had been caught in the rain during break and were now gently steaming on the anxious bodies of hormonal teenagers. I didn't want to be there with all my might. Everyone was too loud as they bustled in and found the seats that had, unspoken, become theirs over that school term. The social sophistication involved in establishing and maintaining that seating plan was impressive on its own before considering that the same thing was happening in every single classroom throughout the building. My seat was by the radiator and the window. On colder days the left-hand side of my body would become white hot, while my head, which remained level with the vast single-pane window above the sill, would go numb from the cold. I didn't mind this. At least those physical sensations could be relied upon. I knew that they were real, unlike almost everything else that happened in that building.

Our French teacher, Madame Flubert, would enter and immediately shout at everyone to sit still and be quiet. 'Too soon,' I would think. 'Choose your battles, save your energy.' This throng of writhing, pent-up energy and irrational emotion wouldn't settle any faster with her shouting at us. I was always nervous in French. In other classes I could either deflect attention by making everyone laugh or by fielding any questions that might come my way with an innate understanding of the subject, but I didn't understand French. I couldn't learn something as alive as a foreign language by reading off a page, and Madame Flubert didn't share my humour. She also didn't understand that speaking out loud in front of my peers using words I wasn't sure of was a very scary prospect.

I would get my two green French jotters and the copy of *Tricolore 1* out of my wet school bag and spend more time than necessary arranging them, my pens and my pencil case on the tiny desk in front of me. I could feel Anne Harris doing the same behind me and would push my back hard against where the edge of her desk met my seat to make sure her books didn't encroach on my space. Madame Flubert would eventually give up on trying to silence the class and begin teaching over the noise. She would turn to face the chalkboard where she would frantically write something huge and illegible with such vigour that the undersides of her flabby arms assumed a life of their own. The noise levels would remain just shy of fever pitch until eventually she'd wheel around and yell at us with such pitch and force that any human being would have to take notice. Madame Flubert would have just played her trump card and the lesson hadn't have even started. There was now nowhere left for her to go. I felt both exhilarated by the drama and deeply anxious at being a part of it. If the adult in the room didn't have control, then we were all exposed.

I have one very clear memory from that room. Something embarrassing had happened – I don't remember what exactly – but I was white hot with shame. I felt the heat from the radiator sweep through my entire body and I turned my head to the window. I focused hard on the opaque surface of the cold glass where the breath and perspiration of my classmates had gathered. So much had settled there that in places it had formed heavy rivulets that were sliding down to gather on the rotting wooden frame at the window's base. But beyond the glass and my throbbing shame I could still make out the steadying bulk and calm of the Campsie

Fells. The dull day did nothing to dampen their appeal to me just then. I would have given absolutely anything to have been swallowed up in them and away from this room and these people. My insides were swirling, my head reeling. I focused on the smooth, velvety green mass with its grey outcrops resting peacefully on my horizon and I forced memories from the deep recesses of my brain: the gunpowder smell of the granite; the sweet earthiness of the boggy ground. I floundered about in my muddled mind trying to grasp physical sensations: the biting cold of the wind as it forced jagged pinpricks of wet rain into my face. Slowly my vision cleared and I could imagine that my raised heart rate and perspiration were from the exertion of running free and unencumbered over the uneven surface of the hillside. My feet hit the spongy ground without effort or conscious thought then rebounded and found their next placement, sometimes on heather, sometimes on firm grass. A wave of calm certainty came over me. This was real. It might not have been my reality in that moment, but those hills and that grass, the heather and the bog, and the wind and the rain were always there. My place in this classroom was a snapshot in time. These people, who understood nothing and were full of their own insecurities and anxiety, would grow old and die. My anchor points made deep, intuitive sense to me right then. In another world the laughter was fading and I could sense that order was being restored in the place I should have been. But I had gone, and I wasn't coming back.

That's when I started skipping French class and riding into the Campsie Fells instead. Outside the secondary school grounds, a few old friendships from primary school remained. Not deep and long-lasting friendships, but easy, companionable ones with three boys from families whose mothers all knew each other. Barry, Martin and Alasdair were not the popular boys at school, but they all had a quiet self-assurance and a steady moral code. I felt safe and accepted in their company where our common language was not about romance, make-up or school subjects but about mountain biking. These boys had really embraced the identity of 'mountain bikers' and they expressed themselves by wearing special padded shorts and garish Lycra tops. They saved up their pocket money and bought themselves Giro helmets, Nike Poobah shoes and copies of *Mountain Biking UK*, things I had no idea would one day hold a similar appeal for me. To begin with, the thing that I most coveted was the confidence they seemed to have in their ability to reach the Campsie Fells and return home before dark.

The Campsies were somewhere I'd been taken a lot as a child (my dad having grown up in them), but I had always been driven there to go walking or to guddle in rivers while my parents drank pints in beer gardens. I'd never considered the idea that I might be able to get there by pedalling a bike and it took this little group of kind, gentle boys to show me the way. I was thirteen years old and I was about to be given a lifeline.

On a bright Friday morning in October when we should have been in French class, Barry, Martin, Alasdair and I stuffed our pockets with biscuits, tied rain jackets around our waists and rode out of Lenzie to Kirkintilloch to find the old railway line that would take us to the foot of the Campsies. I was tingling with excitement and blissfully unaware of just how hard this ride was going to be. This magical stolen time and the defiant camaraderie of four unlikely adventurers was enough to drown out the persistent hum of doubt. The climb up the Tak Ma Doon Road was the hardest thing I had ever done. I arrived at the top the same shade of puce as was common in mountain bike apparel at the time. We then clocked up forty miles per hour (according to Martin's bar-mounted speed-ometer) on our descent into the Carron Valley. We were twenty-five miles into the ride and now on the other side of the hills, completely committed to carrying on to Fintry where we would pick up the infamous Crow Road to return us to the right side of the hills for home. I don't remember much detail of the ride after the descent into the Carron Valley, but I remember that hunger and utter exhaustion had fully set in by that time. I dimly recollect the boys chatting amiably ahead of me while I hung on to their wheels for dear life and fought down my panic at being so far from home in this wild place under my own steam. I remember the wind lifting and turning to face us as we battled our way back over to Lennoxtown, the long, buff marram grass flattened almost completely against the ground on the roadside verge. When we finally reached the edge of Kirkin-tilloch, my friends still had the energy to smile and say goodbye as we parted company to ride to our respective homes. I summoned something approaching civility from a place of egotistical necessity before taking my leave and then, when out of sight of the others, began crawling home alone.

Despite my near comatose state, this is when the memories of that ride start in earnest. Dusk was settling on the hedgerows that lined the path I rode along. It was a route I had walked countless times before with family on dog walks or solo explorations as a child, but that evening everything looked completely different. My whole way of relating to the world around me had tilted on its axis. The trail was narrower and shorter than my memory could allow me to believe. My world had shrunk. The colours of the turning leaves were popping out of their forms and dancing before my eyes in a vague orange haze, but the standing of trees I had once considered grand seemed smaller, parochial. As the sun sank in the clear sky, broadening its wide smile, I got the feeling this sunset was just for me. My body felt utterly depleted. My bum hurt so much that I could no longer sit down, nor could my legs sustain me. Sheer willpower was insisting I pull and push my way through three revo-lutions of the pedals, freewheel until almost stationary then repeat. I was ravenous and chilled to the bone, but I was utterly ecstatic at what was happening to me. In the space of seven hours, I had discovered something about my physicality in relation to wild, remote places that I hadn't even known to dream of before.

Mountain biking would continue to weave a silver thread through the tangled web of my adolescence. Long rides would be something I returned to again and again, sometimes with those boys but more often alone. I would ride until I got lost, led into uncharted territory by the blue and red signs that marked the National Cycle Network, then find a train station and use public transport to get home. These secret explorations gave me back some of my child-hood confidence and a renewed sense of self. I was still counting down the days until I could leave school and start becoming who I felt I really was, but meanwhile discovering what my body was capable of on a bike was transformative. My emerging physicality was like fairy dust I could sprinkle over the chrysalis of my teenage caterpillar. What emerged was a strong, straight-backed, smiling young woman who found herself with an urge to go further into even wilder, more remote landscapes and, most surprisingly of all, to grow her hair.

CHAPTER 3
CYCLETHERAPY

It's incredibly important to me that I'm aware of the shadows cast by my childhood so that I remain aware of how they motivate me to act as an adult. Without this understanding, I risk unthinkingly playing out those traumas in later life. On the other hand, it's an awareness of these dark, uncomfortable, vulnerable, shadowy shapes that motivates and informs our adult lives and, in my case, my career choice. Working with young people suffering the same discomfort and vulnerability I did as a child felt instinctive, and my intensive training in, first, outdoor education and latterly child and adolescent psychotherapy helped me to unpack what was my childhood baggage and what belonged to the young people I was working with. After graduating I worked with several outdoor-focused youth organisations that offered young people the opportunity to play and learn about themselves through adventurous activities. The transformational time I spent as an adolescent riding my mountain bike in the Campsie Fells undoubtedly made me wish for similar therapeutic experiences for other young people struggling to find their place in the world, but I was keen not to force my own agenda and solutions on to those I came into contact with. Outdoor adventure experiences had been my tonic, but it felt more appropriate to meet these kids where they were comfortable. As a result, my employment became less and less about the outdoor activities and more and more about the young people themselves, which is why I found myself working with some of the harder-to-reach kids in schools across the Highlands. Schools were where the kids could be found (unless they were skipping class to ride bikes in the local hills!), so that was where I chose to base myself.

I lasted three years at the Highland Council's Pupil Support Service before I couldn't contain my own childhood baggage any longer. Schools were not where my inner child could thrive when working with these kids.

No one at the Highland Council believed I would quit my well-paid, permanent contract, so when I did hand in my notice it was received with surprise. I was leaving a good, safe job with a pension and a healthy monthly salary, but I had started to notice that there was a staleness in the work I was doing with the young people referred to me. Most of my teaching colleagues were committed to their contracts and some confessed they would never quit because they had big mortgages and families to support. Most of them really cared about the children they were teaching, but other than that, there was no incentive for them to try something new or challenge the educational system that was failing so many of the young people on the Pupil Support Service case load. Complacency had taken root and the bare minimum was taking place so that an easy life could be had by all.

Accompanying the freedom found in leaving a constraining job or a demanding relationship is the shadow of fear and uncertainty. Freedom is exhilarating, and from it creativity and learning flow, but knowing that isn't always enough to stare these dark shadows in the face.

They say that the years speed up as you get older because what makes time move more slowly is exposure to new experiences. Once we settle into our ways of being, whether that's staying in one place, starting a family or settling into a familiar job, the uncomfortable feelings of fear and uncertainty no longer feature in the same way as they might for a child who is constantly exploring and playing in order to make sense of a new and complicated world. For a child, a day might as well be a week if something longed for is at the other end of it. We rarely suffer the same time torture when we become adults, nor do we feel the same excitement for things as often. Routine and familiarity can cause our adult days to trundle amicably by until one day we wake up and wonder where life has gone. I sometimes feel grown-up life can be characterised by saying, 'After these next few weeks things will calm down a bit' over and over again until we reach old age. By always taking the easy road or by filling up all the spaces, we give up the opportunity to experience that wonderful moment when fear or boredom give way to exhilaration or understanding. Stepping off that ledge, leaving that shore, giving up that house, that job: these are hard things to do and made harder still if your bank of fond memories associated with them has swollen with time. But in my experience, it's always been worth it and leaving my job with the council was no exception.

I can remember now the feel of school staffrooms at break, tired teachers clutching instant coffees and dunking custard creams while telling each other bad-luck stories or searching for collusion from their colleagues about the bad behaviour of certain pupils. These rooms with their scratchy chairs, Victorian heating systems and complicated codes of conduct felt stifling to me. As a visitor to secondary schools across the Highlands, it was my job to base myself in several of them for half a day a week and work one-to-one with their most disengaged pupils. I'd enter a staffroom in the morning to find mouths turned down and life left at the main gates. Small rituals were clung to in these rooms as though the world depended on them to keep turning. There were strict rules about which cup I could use and where I could sit, and more subtle ones about eye contact and conversation topics that I always seemed to get wrong.

Schools have never felt like very safe places to me. With many pupils (and teachers!) just surviving in them, there has never felt like there is much room to extend compassion or understanding to one another. As a pupil, my best bet was to approach every social situation by defending myself or with fists flailing, but this defensiveness was hard to keep up for seven hours a day, five days a week, which was why retreating to toilet cubicles or ducking out the back gates instead of attending certain classes became essential survival techniques to me as a teenager. But as an adult working in schools that kind of behaviour wasn't really acceptable.

The kids that were referred to the Pupil Support Service were the ones causing most disruption in class, the fourteen and fifteen-year-old boys whose wonderfully wired brains just wouldn't let them settle into the classroom environment and who had to keep rebelling in case they were rejected by their peers. They'd swagger down to my room then knock shyly on the door. This always touched me: that they would come of their own free will to be in a one-to-one space with me for forty-five minutes and that by doing so they were allowing me the opportunity to reach them wherever they might be. Of course it meant they might miss maths, which, for most of them, was a very appealing prospect, but after the first session with me these boys knew that a one-to-one wasn't the easy option. I had 'work' I was supposed to do with them – anger management, relaxation, conflict resolution, restorative conversation – but unless these boys bought into these processes there was absolutely no point in beginning them. Their buying into a process would only come after they had recognised an issue and wanted to change it for themselves and so this was the first piece of work we shared, and what we'd come up with together was rarely the same issue as the one senior management had referred them for. Anger, frustration, hyperactivity: these were the issues school staff wanted dealt with so they could do their jobs more easily, but these were just manifestations of fear, sadness or insecurity, and working with those issues is a very different process.

These bored, angry young men would meet me in tiny, stuffy rooms in the support departments of secondary schools across Inverness to 'talk about their emotions'.

'How are you?'

'Fine.'

'What's been the best thing that's happened to you today?'

'… [shrug]'

'Did you have breakfast?'

'[nod]'

'Do you want to take a look at this patronising worksheet designed to help you explore your anger?'

It wouldn't have worked for me either. I hated those rooms, those worksheets, the bell, the corridors reeking with the sour smell of low-level fear. But these fourteen-year-old boys did come to school to attend my sessions and, against all the odds, the forty-five minutes spent in each other's company once a week were splattered with specks of gold. The hint of a smile when James won a hand at Uno, the apple accepted by Josh and the subsequent minutes spent crunching together staring out of the window. The unexpected animation David quite suddenly displayed when I showed some interest in his love for Warhammer. When I remembered just to be with them in that space and to offer them my attention instead of driving an agenda set by the institution that had already failed them, then things felt worthwhile and our relationships developed.

Then one day, during a restorative intervention between a pupil and teacher where it was my job to negotiate getting the pupil back into class after some disruptive behaviour had resulted in expulsion, the teacher said to me, 'Look, Lee, put it in front of me and I'll teach it, but don't ask me to have a relationship with it.'

The following day I handed in my notice as Pupil Support Service Worker.

I had moved away from outdoor education into behavioural support because I was emotionally exhausted from leading groups of children up hills or down rivers and was choosing to spend my energy enjoying the outdoors on my own terms for a change. I was mountain biking a lot in the Highlands at the time and this regular connectedness to wild places combined with the physical exertion was making me very happy and content within myself. I'd noticed how some pupils' ears, deaf to anger management workshops, would prick up in excitement when I began talking about mountain biking, and it helped with initial engagement when senior management told them the school counsellor was also the Scottish Mountain Bike Champion. So, on the back of my resignation as school counsellor, I drafted a proposal to the Area Education Office that included reference to my outdoor education background and my mountain bike leader qualifications and suggested these failing one-to-one sessions be moved out-of-doors. I would leave the Pupil Support Service and set up as a self-employed 'cycletherapist' instead.

I knew if I didn't do this now I risked being ground down by the same institutionalised expectations that were squeezing the life out of the boys being referred to me. I didn't want that for anyone and so Cycletherapy was born: a one-to-one project using mountain bike riding and bike mechanics to provide an alternative education opportunity. At least that's what the proposal said. Ostensibly, Cycletherapy was a way to get these boys outdoors and active so they might learn ways to regulate their own emotions through exercise, understand realistically how to assess risk and, above all, be given the opportunity to develop a real, trusting relationship with an adult who wasn't always having to tell them what to do. It was a project aimed at untangling the narrative they had been told their whole lives: that who they were just wasn't good enough. Almost all the boys referred to me were at risk of being excluded from school for displaying signs of attention deficit hyperactivity disorder (ADHD). Since I set up Cycletherapy there has been an exponential rise in ADHD diagnosis in children and adults alike. In a radical reframing of this social problem, Florence Williams suggests that this generation of ADHD sufferers might be our saviours. In her book *The Nature Fix*, Williams suggests that we all need movement and exploration to learn and grow but that our move indoors and our trend towards more sedentary behaviours is killing our natural creativity and curiosity. If we take a horse or a dog out of their natural environment and force them into stables or concrete compounds, neurotic behaviours develop. This isn't the animal's fault. It's the disconnect between their environment and their nature that causes these behavioural problems. The boys I was working with saw the world differently and reminded me daily that we are all on this spectrum and that we all need time to play in unstructured ways.

I don't learn by being sat down and told what to do either. I have to work things out for myself and the only way I learn anything in a meaningful way is if there are consequences to getting it wrong.

It used to be that a child would grow up in a remote glen and intrinsically learn what they needed to know before they ventured on to the hill. Weather patterns, seasons, the rising and falling of water levels, the significance of wind direction, contours, ground cover, distance, day length, colours of vegetation and the varying sounds of the stag: all of this wasn't taught in a classroom. Now we learn it by reading books, going on training courses or trawling the internet. We educate ourselves by studying maps and weather forecasts. We insulate ourselves, with our warm, waterproof clothing, from the elements; from the very things that are trying to tell us something. We think ourselves evolved, and perhaps we are in some ways, but are we better equipped now to enter the hills than that child who had grown up understanding intuitively when and how to venture away from the homestead? Is it evolved to ignore nature's warnings and push on regardless to claim summits or set records despite the weather or season by using specialist equipment, technology and training? It's something, but I'm not sure it's evolved. From some angles it might look brave and impressive, but from others, completely ridiculous.

Most of us have lost our way a little when it comes to taking risks. Some take more than their fair share while others are insulated from the very idea. This is especially true where our children are concerned. I'm not sure how we ever expect children to discover their capabilities if they are not allowed to reach the edge of their ability and lose their balance, skin their knees or cope with getting muddy. It can be painful to watch someone we love stumbling towards a fall, but I wonder if it's more dangerous for us not to allow them that sort of essential learning which will serve them in the long run. In the world of outdoor adventure there's something else going on too. Those of us with degrees in outdoor education or qualifications in leading others in the hills often speak in ways that set our wild places on the top shelf, out of the reach of those who do not yet know what we know and wear what we think is appropriate. It takes time to understand the nuances of a 1:50,000 map and compass, and it's reputed to be dangerous to venture into wild places without Gore-Tex and gaiters. Yet how many of us are evolved enough to sniff the air and feel what the wind might do later that day? How many of us have learned a landscape inch by progressive inch over decades so that we know when and how to retreat to safety storm-blind? Might it be true that maps and expensive equipment have made us dull?

Visiting students from the Czech Republic landed in Ambleside a few years ago on a student exchange, sent from their university's outdoor education programme in order to understand what makes a competent outdoor leader in the UK. These students thought maps were a strange concept. In their country, the military are the only ones to have access to mapping; everyone else follows waymarkers and asks other people for directions or uses landmarks along the way for navigation. The visiting students were in the UK to see how to do things 'properly' and to learn to act 'responsibly', but what does this mean? Responsible behaviour in the outdoors means different things in different cultures. As a member of a mountain rescue team and lifelong hill-goer I've seen plenty of mistakes made, some of them life-threatening – and some of them by me. It's a fine interplay educating, instructing and facilitating outdoor experiences for others, but developing other people's judgement is rarely top of the list of learning outcomes. If we waymarked trails in the Lake District the way they do in many other countries, maybe more people would access our hillsides safely enough to then understand the importance of relearning the things many of us knew deep down hundreds of years ago but that we have lost touch with over time. Maybe by making these places more accessible to more people we allow more people to feel connected to, and worthy of, a relationship with nature. Perhaps too much knowledge and ready access to expensive equipment means we miss the point of being in the mountains. That said, I love my Gore-Tex jacket and I wouldn't go anywhere without it. I do draw the line at gaiters, though.

My return to working with young people in the outdoors felt like a homecoming. For four fulfilling years I would pick up excluded pupils from their home or social work department and drive them out of town to one of the several mountain bike trails Inverness has to offer. Often on the drive out of town, no words would be exchanged, but contact in some form or other would always have been made by the time we parked up. I'd get two very nice, top-spec sponsored mountain bikes out of my van then I'd lead them on a ride on which they controlled the speed and direction. Some of the trails I took the boys on were deliberately hard. I would assess the potential for injury on a particular section and then, if it wasn't high, allow them to make up their own minds about whether or not they rode it. In the four years Cycletherapy operated I can think of only one occasion when a boy rode something he wasn't skilled enough for. In every other instance, these young men, who were often feared by teaching staff due to their volatile behaviour, would calmly assess the terrain and either get off and walk or make a plan to ride the feature safely. In those moments I'd wait to be asked for my opinion on whether I thought they could ride a section of trail and then only offer instruction if pressed further. The quality of these exchanges felt more valuable than anything I ever achieved in those one-to-one rooms.

After a two-hour session, muddy, tired and satisfied, we'd return to Inverness in my van and it was here the magic often happened. With eyes facing forward, the rumble of the engine filling the space between us and with no expectation that they 'talk about their feelings', invariably, they would do just that. So regularly, in fact, that I began extending the van journey back to their school or home to give them the time they needed to say the words that had built up over the session, the week, the year, sometimes even their lifetime.

Inverness, in the heart of the Highlands of Scotland, has a population of fewer than 50,000 but it contains an area listed as the eighth most deprived out of 7,000 locations across Scotland. There were multiple families in this area whose anti-social behaviour had been recorded by police for generations and who were well known to social services. They were dubbed 'troubled'. It was generally thought that kids growing up in these households wouldn't amount to anything and that they would probably follow in the footsteps of their fathers and end up with a drug or alcohol addiction and in prison. When they were referred to me I would read their social work report and attend meetings that usually consisted of professionals giving an update on their behaviour in the community, followed quickly with their opinion on what was good for the young offender. While it's true that a young person and their parent or caregiver were given the opportunity to speak at these meetings, it was rare that they did. They were intimidating places and the meetings often used language not always shared with the families we were supposedly there to help. Often we'd assemble around a cheap Formica table in an austere, windowless room with a suspended polystyrene ceiling and flaking wallpaper in a social work department without any public transport to its door. Caregivers were defensive and sulky. Young people were scared and angry. Stressed social workers, overworked guidance teachers and imposing police officers sat tight-lipped, barricaded behind piles of case notes in dog-eared ring binders. I was invited to these meetings as a named player in a Child's Plan. I always felt repulsion at the prospect of attending but I always did, my reluctance being a fraction of that felt by the family who had been summoned to be judged.

I had worked with Colin once a week for almost a year when I received a request to attend an emergency panel meeting to discuss his 'extremely concerning risk-taking behaviours'. This was bad news. Colin was on his final warning with social work. He had already been removed from his family home and placed in residential care at the children's home in Dingwall, twenty miles from Inverness. The next move would be a secure unit in Glasgow or Edinburgh. I was confused. Colin had been on really good form lately. We'd ridden some challenging mountain bike routes around his new home in Dingwall and he had always risen to the challenge and remained full of humour and enthusiasm, even when things got frustrating. We'd talked about past traumas and current fears. He'd been open about his aspirations to become a bike mechanic and to ride long distances self-supported one day. As far as I knew, Colin was keeping his head down and was attending school on a reduced timetable most weeks. I couldn't get any more information about the risk-taking behaviours he was alleged to have been involved in and I wasn't due to see him before the hearing, so I put it in my diary and out of my head so that I could concentrate on the rest of my case load until we were due to meet.

On the date of the Child's Plan meeting I turned up as I usually did on my muddy mountain bike and brought it into the window-less room to counteract the oppressive blanket of officialdom before it closed Colin down completely. Colin had heard me approach from the other end of the corridor as I sheepishly wheeled in, wincing at the horrible grating noise coming from the front brake caliper. He leapt to his feet and took great pleasure in showing his mum that he knew what was making the sound and explained how it could be fixed. It didn't take a bike mechanic to work that out, but I was glad he felt he had some superior knowledge in that room, even if only for a few minutes. Colin's social worker called the meeting to order and we all sat down on our plastic chairs. A heavy silence fell, propped up only by the hum of the strip lighting. Colin sat slumped low in his seat, chin, mouth and nose tucked so deeply into his jacket that it was a wonder he could still breathe. His hands were thrust so forcefully into his pockets that I could see the material straining.

'Right. Thank you for coming, everyone ... '

We all zoned out a little to the bored tones of this tired social worker as she went through the motions of setting up the meeting legally. She was a good one. She'd battled to keep Colin in the High-land region when he'd been taken into care so that contact could be maintained with his mum who was suffering from depression. She had also made the referral to Cycletherapy, understanding that he might benefit from a physical, practical focus to counteract the boredom he was feeling following his exclusion from school. This social worker was doing the best job she could given she was exhausted and hamstrung by the system in which she was operating.

'... so I think you'll agree that absconding from a curfewed care home in Dingwall and riding a bike twenty miles to Inverness in the dead of night is unacceptably risky behaviour that must be addressed.'

I cast a glance at Colin who held my gaze just long enough to communicate the smile that was obviously happening behind his jacket. I looked away and down at my dirty hands. My mind was whirling, but with what? Guilt? Concern? I knew these were the things the other professionals in the room would be expecting me to feel, but in my heart I couldn't honestly put my finger on these as my primary emotions. No. To my alarm I realised that I was going to have to look up into the eyes of these statutory service workers and control the size of my grin. My heart was about to burst with admiration and pride at the feat of physical and emotional resilience Colin had shown by riding that kind of distance on a bike he had built with his own hands.

This boy had been referred to me with low self-esteem and anxiety manifesting in drug-taking and violent behaviours. He had been unwilling to ride a bike anywhere at first, and so we had spent week after week in the bike workshop stripping down and rebuilding a bike from the reclaimed carcasses of recycled ones. After two months spent drinking tea and fiddling with bikes we had established enough mutual trust for Colin to agree to come on a short bike ride with me. We didn't go far that first day, but we did have fun. We rode along the canal and into some woods where we practised skidding in the mud, only returning to my van filthy and happy with pink cheeks and shaky legs when the light began to fade. By the time I dropped him at the residential centre he was reluctantly calling home, we had already planned the following week's ride.

For the next year Colin and I steadily ticked off all the local mountain bike trails in the area, and he learned how to navigate roads and other vehicles each week, going further and faster as his confidence grew. Then one day he asked me how long I thought it would take him to ride to Inverness. We got the map out and I showed him that there was a National Cycle Network route between Dingwall and Inverness, and he worked out that it would probably take at least two hours of solid riding to complete.

Over the past year, Colin had gone from being someone unfit from a weed and PlayStation addiction to someone motivated and able to ride a self-built mountain bike more than twenty miles in order to reconnect with the people he loved.

The room was very hot. I had to make a rapid calculation before I looked up. I was going to have to either acknowledge my respect for Colin and lose the alliance I required with his referrer to continue working with him, or suppress the deep joy I could feel rising in my throat and put on a stern face. I squeezed my left hand hard with my right and resolved to aim for something between the two, but it was pointless. I lifted my head and burst out laughing.

Colin and I continued to work together after that meeting for another year before he was eventually convicted of assault and moved out of the area. He told me once that he wanted to go to prison because that's what the men in his family had always done. It was his rite of passage to adulthood. My heart sank when I heard this and I cried when I heard his conviction had finally taken place. When I think of Colin now I remember a round, smiling, intelligent face with cheeks that would turn pink when he said a word wrong or when he would sing along to the radio in my van. I remember large, competent, gentle hands that intuitively knew what to do with a set of Allen keys but that would sit clenched and white in his lap after a visit home to see his depressed mum and angry older brother. I remember the whoops of joy he would make as we slid down muddy singletrack in the woods above his care home and I find myself to this day making those same noises in similar circumstances. And now, when I remember that glance we shared in Carsegate Social Work offices the afternoon we sat through an emergency meeting about his 'risk-taking behaviours', I get a lump in my throat. The lump is joy and grief in equal measure. I feel humbled by Colin's sustained empathy for the family that couldn't give him what he needed to thrive and angry for the part the system played in further eroding his feelings of self-worth. This boy had (and still has, hopefully) good humour, creativity, curiosity and ambition in bucketloads. It's memories of time spent with boys like Colin that ensure I never take my eye off the social justice ball in every conversation I have. By and large, our society is not set up to acknowledge the alternative excellence of characters who fall outside our safe, social norms. I feel this strongly and it forms part of the reason I use my white, educated, middle-class privilege now to show a different way to live, one where all you need to be happy is two small bike bags, a stove, a tent, a sense of adventure and, when all else fails, a sense of humour.

CHAPTER 4
THE BRITISH CHAMPIONSHIP

While I was acutely aware that a puncture or a crash might still mean losing this race, after more than an hour on the bike I had begun to entertain the possibility that today I might finally become the British Mountain Bike Champion.

It was a sunny Sunday morning in June 2013 and the battle for the championship title was taking place over five laps of a four-mile course which had been built for the mountain bike competition at the Commonwealth Games the following year. The demanding route had no long climbs but lots of steep, sharp, difficult ones requiring core strength and explosive power to deliver the rider back to the start/finish line at the top of the hill. Here riders were offered a brief respite from the steep terrain and an impressive view over the city of Glasgow, before plunging below the treeline again over rock drops and through twisting singletrack.

When the gun had gone at 10 a.m., thirty highly trained mountain bike racers had sprinted for that first descent, a homogeneous group with a shared understanding that being the first to drop into that singletrack meant not being held up by other riders' mistakes. Working your way back to the lead rider if that happened off the start line was always extra hard and could often take the entire race to achieve.

I suspected it was going to be a good day when, to my surprise, I made it to the first descent half a wheel length ahead of the world downhill and enduro champion, Tracy Moseley. I then battled imposter syndrome at taking the first three-foot drop ahead of her. I could feel Tracy's front tyre grating my rear one most of the way down that first descent and so when the course turned sharply to climb steeply uphill I breathed a sigh of relief, safe in the knowledge that I could create a gap from the rest of the race if I was willing to dig deep and suffer a little.

In the days leading up to this race I had tussled with feelings of constant dread which manifested in a tight chest and churning stomach. It took me years of racing to understand that the part I was dreading the most was not being beaten or falling off and injuring myself. The dread came exclusively from the knowledge that come Sunday morning, things were going to hurt. The pain and discomfort I would feel at the front of a cross-country mountain bike race is almost impossible to put into words, but let me try. I've never experienced discomfort like that felt on a tough climb on lap three of a five-lap race when the lactic acid build-up in my legs would turn them to rubber, my ears would whistle from the lack of oxygen to my brain, my heart would pound the inside of my ribs, my throat would feel scorched and my vision would narrow to a pinprick in the distance. At this point in a race, every single cell in my body would scream at me to *stop*, and yet success, we are told, lies in ignoring that command and pressing on through the pain.

When described in this way, participating in endurance sport sounds very unhealthy, but it edges towards barbaric when we consider that sporting success means putting yourself through all of that so you might beat other people. I dedicated ten years of my life to getting faster on a bike so that I could beat other people over a finish line. This dedication was a lifestyle choice. Decisions about whether to walk up a hill with friends, accept a piece of birthday cake or go to a party were made using the same criterion: 'Will this make me go faster on a bike?' If the answer was no then I wouldn't do it (or if I did do it then I wouldn't enjoy it). I became paranoid about getting ill or injured and I was constantly stressed about fitting in my training alongside the other commitments in my life.

My racing ambitions meant sacrificing every weekend to drive long distances, often with my generous partner, Ferga, who would stand in cold feed zones to pass me bottles each lap. When I look back on everything we must have both missed out on as a result of my racing, I feel very humbled by her selflessness.

I did try and strike a balance. Over time I got better at prioritising some races over others and built in time around the less important ones to socialise and give something back to Ferga, my friends and family. On one attempt to balance my racing and social life I agreed to go to Knockengorroch Festival in Dumfries and Galloway. I thought I could party soberly during the day and go to bed relatively early each night. I'd then leave on Sunday morning in time to compete at a nearby Scottish Cross Country Mountain Bike Series race in Dalbeattie. I had a great weekend listening to music, dancing and catching up with old friends and went to bed about midnight on Saturday leaving Ferga and Alison dancing wildly, partially naked and covered in body paint. In the morning I packed my van and organised my race equipment then went to find my support crew. Ferga and Al were still dancing. Despite this, and only thirty minutes later than planned, Ferga and Al were in my van and we were on our way to Dalbeattie. I pulled into the car park where the same familiar athletic forms I saw at every Scottish race were already warming up on static bikes next to their vehicles. I parked next to them and opened the back of the van. The smell of booze wafted out and my support team toppled sideways from the cab still covered in body paint but also, inexplicably, in straw and glitter. They stood blinking in the brutal sunlight of the wholesome day, looking for all the world like they had been spirited there from another planet. I thought about asking one of them to sign on for me so I could begin my warm-up then thought better of it and moved in the direction of race HQ to do it myself. When I returned, everything was exactly as I'd left it, except Ferga and Al were missing and so were my bottles for the feed zone. I had to trust that they would be there when I came round needing a bottle after my first lap.

It was pointed out on the start line that morning that my mascara had run. I told my competitors that if they thought I looked like I'd been dragged through a hedge backwards then they should wait and see the state of my support crew when we hit the feed zone. We set off on the gun and twenty minutes later, the first feed zone came into view. Ferga and Al were recognisable at least (their outfits now embellished by tweed flat caps and mysterious feather boas that I hadn't seen before), but their coordination was off and I missed the bottle they held up. Later in the lap, Ferga popped up apologetically and out of breath to try and hand it to me again, but there are rules against accepting a bottle outside feed zones. I barked, 'Not here!', and sped off. I was at the front of the race and pretty focused, so the next time I came through the feed zone I tried again to take the bottle and explain what sustenance I might need on the following lap. I usually took a gel on my penultimate lap, but this morning I needed more than that, so I tried to tell them to pass me up some real food next time. I had enough time to register blank, pale faces before I charged off again. When I came round for the final time, there was a deafening roar from the feed zone. More of my friends had left the festival and found their way to Dalbeattie. They stood in a bedraggled line in the feed zone holding bags of Jelly Babies, half-eaten Pot Noodles, beer, veggie burgers, packets of salt and vinegar crisps and a Super Soaker water pistol. As I approached feeling humbled and amused, they sang in unison, 'Not here?' It was a lesson in not taking myself too seriously that would serve me incredibly well in the years to come.

Competitive sport could bring out the very worst in me, but the brutal simplicity of physical competition was also a very honest and pure thing to commit wholeheartedly to. Growing up in the shadow of my older sister, I tried to convince myself that my physical competency was something I needed to prove just to myself, but what racing taught me was that unless we grow up in complete isolation from the rest of the human race, or evolve spiritually beyond comprehension, there is an element of comparison with others that hatches from the same place as our survival instinct. Bike racing was my way to square up to this ugly aspect of my humanity. The dark places in us are only dangerous if we don't acknowledge them.

It's always been interesting to me that elite sport is held in such high regard when if you scratch below the very impressive surface what often gets revealed are obsessive compulsive disorders, fanaticism, selfishness and egotistical ambition. We are rightly impressed by an athlete's dedication and discipline and inspired by their physical prowess, so much so that it can encourage us all to achieve in our own way. I am personally very grateful to Boris Becker and Ivan Lendl whose legendary status in my neighbourhood meant that every summer when Wimbledon dominated our media, all the kids in my street developed their hand-eye coordination by hitting balls at each other. We are taught to admire sportspeople and, as children, to emulate them, but the world of sport is an extreme and uncompromising place for a young person to form a set of values. You win or you lose and there are repercussions to both.

Achieving success in life is often associated with having money, fame or influence, but imagine a world where kindness and patience are valued over any other attributes traditionally associated with success. In a world like this our nurses and support workers would be paid more than our investment bankers and politicians. Now imagine a sporting competition where this might also be true. By the time I was racing in the 2013 British Mountain Bike Championships I had begun to acknowledge that patience and kindness might hold the secret to better managing the pain that I dreaded so much in the days preceding a race. I had been applying the basic principles of Buddhist philosophy to bike racing and it was helping me reframe my experience. Pain multiplied by resistance equals suffering, so I had begun experimenting with what happens if I multiply pain with love instead. I can tell you that the result is still a lactic acid build-up, but something else happens too. I know sending out love to counteract resistance sounds far-fetched, especially having described how much I was physically suffering, but I have always been fascinated by the difference between physical and emotional pain. I'd remind myself that my body was designed to function like this. That within it, there was a vast vault of wisdom that I would probably never understand but that I would be okay. I'd shut out the fear ('What if my heart explodes?!') but acknowledge the pain with love and kindness. I'd self-soothe by channelling the calm I could generate to areas of my body where panic had gripped the sinew and was halting performance. While still squeezing out the effort I'd look up and pull my breath further into my lungs. I'd take that sharp stabbing pain in my neck and focus on it until the edges of it grew fuzzy. I'd smile. That was hard. It took energy to smile and these were non-essential muscle movements, but in doing so I'd release tension elsewhere in my body which in turn seemed to free up blockages of energy to my rubber legs and rasping lungs. Sometimes, by doing all of this I'd experience a surge of forward motion in those moments, but often, these gentle thoughts would simply help more moments pass by where my pain hadn't been my entire reality. It was the blissed-out wonder I felt at having caught a glimpse into the seemingly limitless landscape of the physical and mental potential of the human being that kept me going.

Every woman on the start line at Cathkin Braes that July morning had extremely high levels of all-round fitness and bike-handling ability and, while I'm not suggesting there weren't some more physiologically trained than others, I firmly believe that what separated our performances the most was our individual emotional responses to pain. This sounds simple and I don't mean to devalue all the hard physical conditioning that goes into becoming an elite-level athlete. Years of physiological conditioning cannot be replaced by learning to emotionally manage pain better, but understanding the extent to which it is possible to compartmentalise pain and still do the thing that is causing the discomfort is a game changer. I wonder if those who are willing to stay open to new knowledge and not shy away from the hard stuff tend to grow and learn at a different rate from those who never leave their comfort zone?

Now, at just after 11 a.m., on the final climb to the finish line on the last lap of the British championship race, I was finally, tentatively, allowing myself to believe that I might be about to win the coveted championship title. The relief and euphoria had already begun to bubble uncomfortably in my parched throat and the whistling in my ears from oxygen deprivation was no longer distinguishable from the roar of the crowd. As I rolled over the line with both arms in the air to the applause of a home crowd delighted that a Scot would hold the British title in the run-up to the Commonwealth Games, a gust of wind took my front wheel and I very nearly crashed. Another timely reminder to stay humble.

The year I became British Mountain Bike Champion, I'd been racing seriously for six years. I was training for up to six hours a day following a strict plan that included bike and gym work, skills practice and a detailed diet. I had a bike and equipment sponsor, and Scottish Cycling paid my expenses to attend races, which were almost every weekend between May and October. I had always ridden a mountain bike, but this level of commitment to competition had crept up on me. When I had moved to the Highlands ten years previously, I'd used my bike to explore the more remote areas of Torridon, Fisherfield, the Cairngorms and Kintail with my friend Tony. Those long days spent carrying and pushing our bikes as much as riding them on rough walking trails had trained my body and mind to be strong. As a result, when the Scottish Cross Country Mountain Bike Series race came to Contin near my home, I entered it out of curiosity and, to my surprise, I won. Many of my competitors in that race had been nurtured into bike racing as children, whereas my childhood had been spent pretending I was Michael Knight from *Knight Rider* and his car Kit was my small red BMX. Despite my win I felt I had left it too late to compete at anything close to a high level in the sport. There was a set route to competing at elite level in mountain biking and I hadn't taken it at a young enough age. It's in telling ourselves life-limiting stories like these that opportunities for adventure get missed. It took some reframing of this narrative and a few more decent results at local level before I finally realised I had all the experience necessary to compete at a high level if that was what I wanted. I was twenty-six years old when I decided this was the direction I wanted to take my life in. Eight years later, I would become the British Champion, but those eight years were to be a steep and uncomfortable learning curve.

In order to progress in any sport, it's imperative that an athlete is given opportunities to do so. This means that once a rider becomes a big fish in a small, local pond, they must step up to national and then international level. Cycling in the UK is a comparatively well-funded sport. British Cycling attracts public money based on the number of medals it wins at major events and this money gets reinvested in its athletes. The problem is, while medals are available in several track cycling disciplines, only single gold, silver and bronze medals are up for grabs in cross-country mountain biking and so to get on to that funded programme is hard. Now throw into the mix an athlete who is pushing thirty and whose travel and subsistence costs are huge – because she lives in the Highlands of Scotland. She's also a complete rocket, publicly open about her unconventional training methods and with a mind of her own. Furthermore, although she consistently finishes elite-level national competitions in first or second place, she didn't achieve that level of prowess through the British Cycling model. Her success doesn't bring with it much kudos to the national governing body of the sport. Scottish Cycling was prepared to really fight my corner and get me on to the support package that would allow me British Cycling support at international events, but first I had to prove I could hold my own on a world stage.

In 2010 I decided that the only way to prove this would be to travel to Europe as a privateer (someone without sponsorship or governing body support) in my van. My friend Tony agreed to come with me and help with the driving and stand in the pits surrounded by uniformed mechanics and branded vehicles to pass my bottles to me. I sought bike and equipment support from Scottish suppliers. The bikes and clothing available to me at the time were too big for me. The bike industry had not yet caught up with the idea that more and more women were mountain biking at the top level and the best bikes were only available in men's sizing. The factory clothing was also only available in men's cuts and sizes, and so when I began the long drive to the Czech Republic, I had with me a bike that was too big and clothing I had taken to a seamstress in Inverness to adapt for my body shape. This has since changed a lot but not as much as some might think. The bike industry still produces fewer top-end bikes and less clothing for women because 'the market just isn't there'. This, I believe, is at the heart of why more women don't compete in mountain biking. We are told by marketing manufacturers in the industry that we don't belong in the space, and so there is less representation at the top level and therefore fewer role models for young women to look up to. All the same, Team Craigie left Scotland foolishly underprepared to spend six weeks living and racing all over Europe out of a tiny Renault Traffic van. My privilege and a healthy self-confidence made this possible. I had nothing to lose other than a lot of personal money and a good friendship, but I felt that Tony and I had endured enough together in the Scottish Highlands to emerge from this adventure relatively unscathed.

As a result, my first race felt charged with potential vindication. If I could perform under these conditions, then British Cycling would have to take notice of me. It was a liberating and terrifying prospect.

Round one of the World Cup at Nové Město was intimidating in the extreme. As an unknown rider I was gridded right at the very back of a field of seventy-plus international female riders all wearing varying degrees of ill-fitting kit emblazoned with sponsorship logos. I stood astride my oversized bike in the hot sun with my heart hammering waiting for the start gun, but when it sounded, nothing happened. There were so many riders ahead of me that it took several seconds for the field to clear sufficiently for me to find my pedals and start picking my way up through the field. Yet that seemed to be what was happening. I was confidently weaving in and out of other riders until I was sitting comfortably mid-pack. This is important. The start of a world cup is a brutal, limb-flailing affair, but I knew from my practice laps of the course that if I didn't bury myself for the first two minutes I'd be caught in a bottleneck when the track narrowed and entered the technical singletrack in the woods. As a result, I was fully in the red by the time this happened. I may have made vital ground, but I was now seeing stars only 180 seconds into the race. I slackened my pace and allowed a gap to open up between me and the next rider so I could gather myself. The noise of chains grinding over badly found gears and the hollow clang of expensive carbon rims, together with an already well-oiled crowd, filled my head before I eventually found my breath and allowed it to narrow my focus to a pinprick. I found sublime moments of flow on that trail, over rocky features and down steep, twisting, rooty sections. Some women passed me, but I kept the pressure on as best I could. When I came into view of the first technical assistance zone I saw Tony shoved right to the back behind some burly German mechanics waving bottles and surrounded by tables full of spare parts and expensive-looking tools. They were red-faced and shouting at their rider, who lifted a bottle from them at breakneck speed. Tony stood with one hand behind his back, a little mat laid out at his feet with a single multi-tool and track pump lying forlornly on it. I heard him utter a single, subtle 'Go, Lee' as I passed, unable to reach the bottle he was holding up, but it was enough to know that he was there. I set out on lap two of this five-lap course. My world was now a series of increasingly familiar bends and drops and my own heart and lungs. The pain in my legs, neck and forearms was excruciating. The air was burning my throat and my eyes were streaming from the air being forced into them, but I kept the pressure on, revelling in the urgency of the occasion.

A world cup race in 2010 lasted about an hour and a half. That's a long time to be in your own head and it was always interesting to notice where my thoughts would go. In this race I distinctly remember what was rolling around in my mind. I began questioning what it was that had led me to this point. How had I become the sort of person who was willing to impose this level of pain and discomfort on myself? What had possessed me to pack my van, leave my home and drive hundreds of miles across the continent to put myself in this extremely uncomfortable position? As I turned my pedals and this question over and over in my mind, a memory began to replay.

I am four years old and I'm with my family at a dilapidated out-of-season funfair by the sea. There's a narrow-gauge railway with a tiny train made up of three passenger carriages and a little engine. I want to ride that train with every fibre of my being. I'm the only one small enough to be allowed on, so I cast my sister a smug look over the shoulder of my duffle coat as I make my way to the track. When I reach the train I am told I can have my choice of seat. No other children are anywhere to be seen and so without giving it a second thought, I go straight to the little engine and sit behind the wooden wheel. The train starts to move and it's only in that moment that I grab the wheel and focus on the task at hand. I am instantly gripped with fear and pumped full of adrenaline. It's absolutely unfathomable that I've been put in this situation. I'm four years old, for goodness' sake, and I am solely and singlehand-edly responsible for ensuring this entire train doesn't go off the rails. It's picking up speed and I am frantic in my focus. I turn the wee wooden wheel this way and that as the train lurches wildly around corners. I breathe small sighs of relief every time I don't derail and relax my grip ever so slightly on the straight sections of track, but a corner approaches and I summon all my skill and focus to get myself safely around the next bend. The ride goes on forever. I am white hot and desperate for it to be over, but I will not ask for help, I will not panic, I will not cry. At some point after an eternity of wheel turning on high alert I see my family standing behind the white knee-high fence laughing uproariously. I am incensed. Here I am in a fight for my life and all they can do is laugh?! Slowly it dawns on me with a mixture of relief, disappoint-ment and embarrassment that the train is steering itself and that I can let go of the wheel. It's an odd mixture of emotions. Moments before, emerging from the fear were the beginnings of pride and euphoria. I was capable of this. I had been dropped into an unimaginably challenging situation and I was coping with it. I would never have known I was capable of steering this train if I hadn't been dropped into this situation in a massive leap of faith, but it turns out I was!

The strange disappointment that my immense skill and compo-sure hadn't been the reason that train had stayed on its tracks both-ered me, and I was left with an urgent need to rise to another challenge to consolidate my belief that I could achieve the impossi-ble. I reflected, as I raced my heart out around that brutal cross-country mountain bike course in the Czech Republic, that this child-hood experience seemed to have given my adult self free rein to find equally challenging situations so that I could survive them and continue to grow my confidence.

When I rounded into the tech zone for the final time with one lap to go, I saw the British Cycling support team in the pits wearing matching red, white and blue tracksuits. They were there in support of Annie Last, the British number one and the only other British female rider out on course. She was somewhere far, far ahead of me, but when I passed British Cycling's head mountain bike coach, Phil Dixon, he leant forward out of the pits and growled, 'Come on, Lee! Twenty seconds to the next rider.' Until then, I hadn't realised he even knew my name. British Cycling were watching my performance. I felt a surge of renewed energy at the possibility I might finish this race in a reasonable position with Phil watching and I emptied myself entirely on that final lap to finish my first world cup race in a respectable thirty-seventh position.

The next day, after Tony and I had celebrated with a platter of unpronounceable deep-fried food and a vat of Duvel, I got an email from British Cycling. They had been impressed with my out-of-the-blue performance and invited me to ditch my immediate plans and fly to Slovenia for the European Championships. The world cup had felt painful and exhilarating on a level I didn't think was possible, but if I was to improve as a rider then I had to take any opportunity I was offered to race internationally. It was the start I needed.

I was whisked away from my familiar van-based race prep routines and my friend, and ushered to a hotel in rural Slovenia. Beds, meals, massage and supported course practice were all offered to me on a plate. All I had to do was practise riding the course, eat and stretch. When I wasn't doing these things I was encouraged to take the lift up the single flight of stairs to my hotel room, close the curtains against the beautiful blue sky and distant tantalising hills, and lie down. I felt like a cross between a small child and a prize pony, and it made me fidgety and uncomfortable.

The European Championships didn't go so well. It was thirty-eight degrees Celsius on the start line of an uninspiring course that seemed to meander in off-camber grassy lines up and down a steep field. Above us was the horizon of big mountains covered in shady trees, but instead we were racing around this white-hot grassy slope to the incongruous clatter of race-day noise. While my train didn't come off its track entirely that day, it was up on two wheels on a few corners and I was reminded that unless my confidence was allowed to grow at a speed in keeping with the increase in stakes, I stood to fail spectacularly. I had to find my limit and this, it appears, was it. I returned to Tony and the comfort of my shambolic van life in Italy to race a final world cup round which ended slightly better than my Slovenia race. I had learned loads and I was ready for the next season.

When I returned to national-level racing in 2011 I couldn't believe how comfortable and easy it felt. Before my season in Europe these races were overwhelmingly hard, but now my perspective of 'hard' had been shifted. It was what set me up to believe I could win the British championship title and race at international level. In another year, I would stand on a podium at Cathkin Braes in those red, white and blue stripes and feel a lurch of pride.

For a few days after winning the British championship title in 2012 I was delighted with myself. I was floating on a cloud of contentedness and accomplishment. All the hard work had paid off and I could forever lay claim to the red, white and blue bands of British champion. But it wasn't long before those coveted stripes on my jersey reconfigured themselves into concentric circles which formed a target on my back. I was now the one to beat.

I've always been more comfortable chasing than being chased. I'm sure this is to do with the element of control and autonomy available to the chaser and not the chasee. Once at the top, the only direction of travel is back down and everyone colludes with this narrative arc. Underdog rises through the ranks against all the odds and achieves greatness, and then what? Where's the drama in her remaining at the top? And so it was that 2013 became the year of being chased and my fight to cling on to enough resolve to qualify for the 2014 Commonwealth Games. It so nearly didn't happen.

CHAPTER 5
ANDORRA TO THE COMMONWEALTH GAMES

My first international race as British champion was a complete disaster. I'd travelled to Andorra with the Scottish squad, carrying with me the heavy expectation that I would perform well. I didn't. My race was a flop. I was tired and troubled and couldn't find any rhythm on the technical, root-ridden course. My body felt heavy and cumbersome, my bike like a dead weight. I felt my heart rate stubbornly refuse to rise to the level I needed it to and yet I felt sick with fatigue. After the race I couldn't make eye contact with the rest of the squad or with my coach, so that evening I took myself off into the hills in search of some peace and perspective. I was in the High Pyrenees, one of my favourite places in the world with its spectacular ridgelines, glacial rivers and endless trails wiggling through alpine villages and over enticing cols. I had arrived off a carbon-heavy flight on a low-cost airline to sleep in an overheated hotel room to then hate every moment of racing my mountain bike in three-mile circles below a monstrous ski area. If a person doesn't pause to consider their life choices in moments like this, then perhaps they have become removed from what it is that makes life worth living. I was definitely on that path. I was getting a lot from the structure of hard training and working towards my Commonwealth Games goal in 2014, but in that moment I realised this was not going to be enough to sustain me. My racing had become stale

47

and tired. Bike riding usually gave me such joy, but I was struggling to feel anything at all and my relationships were suffering as a result of the focus I needed to stay on the path to the 2014 games.

I decided that instead of flying back with the rest of the squad to continue the relentless race routine, my partner, Ferga, and I would pack our bikes with sleeping bags and stoves, and ride north in the direction of home. Ferga's willingness to adapt to changing circumstances, her deep-rooted spirit of adventure and her self-employed status meant she would often get on board with my impulsive ideas. A few days later, she met me in Andorra.

What followed were some of the best days I've ever had on a bike with another person. Despite both of us having ridden bikes for more than twenty years and having spent extensive periods of time in mountain ranges all over the world, neither of us had ever properly ridden bikes self-supported before, and we had no idea what we were doing. We strapped dry bags everywhere and, hoping for the best, weaved our unbalanced way north towards France. I remember feeling so grateful I was with someone I trusted implicitly. I knew that Ferga and I could handle most things a mountain environment could throw at us, but add to this the uncertainty of how much ground we might be able to cover daily, whether we'd find somewhere to sleep at night that felt safe and where our next meal might come from, and suddenly we were as nervous as children. Before then I'd always met this kind of feeling with more excitement than trepidation, but I didn't have that kind of resilience in me right then. I was tired of fighting. I was worn out and weepy. In those situations, Ferga was my rock. She would watch while I wound myself up for the race season and support me while I held focus, often driving with me all over the country. When I inevitably ran out of steam towards the end of every summer, she would be the one to gently help me unwind and find perspective again. Our personalities were compatible in their differences. While my emotional baseline oscillated like my heart rate – extreme highs followed by extreme lows – Ferga's would flatline – never too high or too low. I could bring her up and together we could get excited about adventures and ideas, then on the way back down, she could soothe us both before I dropped into despair. We made a great team for the fifteen years we spent together.

The daunting ride up through France was not part of the training plan. It was July, mid-race season, and I was narrowly leading the British Series. I was about to throw my training plan out of the window and ride long days, sleep under the stars and sustain myself on croissants and cheese. My coach, Paul, was despairing, but he knew me better than to insist I stick to the plan. He was wise enough to see I was worn out and needed a break. I'm sure Paul would have preferred working with an athlete whose idea of a break was a fully catered beach holiday, but I like to believe I helped him to think laterally.

On our first day out of Andorra, Ferga and I didn't get very far. Our bikes felt awkward and the constant stopping to adjust bags or pick up dropped items meant we never found our flow. We spent ages worrying about where to camp before the gathering dusk forced us to hunker down behind a big boulder in a ski area that obscured us from the road. Having forgotten almost everything of use, including our headtorches, we huddled in our tent and used the beam of a bike light strapped to the bridge of Ferga's glasses to study a road map we had sellotaped together in a garage forecourt that morning. Laid out before us was a network of possibility repre-sented by yellow, orange and white lines squiggling like intestines over steep cols before running straight as beanstalks through open plains. Our eyes were drawn to the green spaces and the areas boasting lakes, rivers and mountains, but we plotted our route north to take in a small town each morning so we could enjoy a morning coffee and buy our supplies for the day to come.

After an evening of silence where our only method of permitted communication was using words spelt out laboriously in alphabet pasta, we slept deeply and woke to frost in the valley. The anxiety from battling the day before with unfamiliar systems and worrying about distance had evaporated with the new day. We waited for the sun to pop up over the mountains, then packed up our bikes while bathed in golden promise for the day that lay ahead. That second day spent moving slowly but purposefully through the Pyrenees on fully laden bikes marked a change in me. For now, at least, all expectation had fallen away. No one was chasing me, I had nowhere to be, the rate at which my heart was beating didn't matter and I could eat whatever I wanted. I stopped caring about getting sick or injured or feeling tired. I was in simple, easy company with someone who loved me regardless of how quickly I could propel a bicycle, and together we were moving through an exquisite mountain landscape, the sun on our faces and the wind on our backs.

For the next two weeks we travelled this way, falling easily into a rhythm with the natural world and each other. We got up when the sun did and swam in the midday heat of it. If the wind picked up or blew the wrong way, we stopped or adapted our route. One day we passed through a village marked with a *Plus Beau Village* sign and were so taken with its quaint beauty that we spent the rest of the day exploring it, pretending to shoot arrows from the slit windows of a fifteenth-century castle and dozing by the river. Afterwards we decided that there were worse ways to choose a bike route than by linking up as many of these historically rich heritage sites as we could find on our road map, so we radically recalculated our journey to take in as many *Plus Beaux Villages* as possible. We wove erratically up through France but never felt hurried or stressed. Leaving one place in order to reach the next one felt pointless when we both felt the moment we were in was the only moment of any real worth.

In the evenings we performed the tasks of setting up camp, washing, cooking and repairing equipment systematically and thoroughly. We would pore over our now ragged road map, reviewing our day and making plans for the next one. A deep sense of satisfaction settled over us as we propelled bikes and bodies not just through space as we followed the lines on a map, but through time as the sun performed its daily magic trick, then handed over to the moon for the night shift. Our bodies adapted to the loads we were carrying and to the constant exposure to the elements, and we grew strong and swarthy while our minds expanded to let in all the luck and chance a journey by bike offers. In letting go of my structured, goal-focused existence and opening myself up to experiencing new things I discovered that good people, perfect camp spots and unexpected swimming holes presented themselves just when we needed them. Travelling without the expectation of discovering any of these things freed us completely of all the self-limiting preconceptions of how things should be that so often trap us in our daily lives. If things felt hard then we stopped; if someone wanted to talk to us we gave them our time, and more often than not, in doing so, we would be gifted a bag of plums or a shady dell in return.

We wound our way up through France via the Cévennes National Park and then the Massif Central, choosing forest roads and singletrack where possible. We grew dirtier, more bedraggled and happier and happier with every passing day.

Objectively, my chances of performing well at the next National Points Series race, having spent two weeks sleeping under the stars, eating my own body weight in cheese and riding from dawn until dusk each day, were not high. Yet on my return to the UK, I went straight into the next race on the calendar wearing the same clothes I had ridden up through France in. I went into that race carrying some of the magic charm from our recent journey and felt, for the first time, not particularly attached to the outcome. My legs were heavy and my skin was nut brown from long days in the sun. My hair was tangled from washing in lakes and rivers and my bike was still covered in dust from the road, but I felt buoyant and lithe. It was a feeling I didn't know had been missing until it was present again, like the feeling you get with the first welcome signs of spring after a long, depressing winter.

To everyone's surprise, not least my own, I won that race and in so doing, claimed the series title and almost guaranteed qualification for the 2014 Commonwealth Games. Coach Paul was bewildered but pleased. The data made no sense to a sports performance coach, but he was humble enough to concede that the complexity of delivering a strong physical performance was not something that sports science has a definitive road map for.

After the race I headed home to Inverness. Inevitably and incrementally I began slipping back into stressed-out behaviours around training and racing as I reset my sights on performing at the games in Glasgow the following year. I knuckled down with British Cycling and Paul to hit power and VO2 max targets, but something had fundamentally shifted in me. On my ride back from Andorra I had felt more content and happy than I had in a long time and I silently resolved that this was the relationship with bikes that I wanted in my future. Something had slackened and relaxed in me with the realisation that my training and lifestyle didn't need to be so prescriptive nor my thinking so tight in order to perform well in races. In fact, there might be such a thing as trying too hard.

When the Commonwealth Games was over, I would travel self-supported by mountain bike and open myself back up to the real world. Meanwhile I could take the experiences that summer and try to apply everything I had learned about cultivating happiness while riding through France to my training and racing.

In the run-up to Glasgow 2014 I balanced my structured training and race commitments with the big mountain adventures of my pre-racing days. I didn't stress as much as I had in the past about my diet and sleep because I had confidence that my body had a wisdom of its own and that it would take what it needed when it needed it. I held on more loosely to any expectations of myself and didn't waste unnecessary energy on stressing about not reaching milestones. I wasn't always completely Zen that year, but I could recognise when stress started piling in and I knew what to do to dissipate it, which was just as well because the selection process for the games was designed to pile as much pressure on us as possible. Every training session, camp or race in early 2014 held an undercurrent of fear. It felt like being back in the school corridors where everyone and everything was a threat and being constantly on the attack was the only way to survive. The idea that your place in Team Scotland could be swiped by someone else was omnipresent. This culture of fear was nurtured by anxious coaches who believed that the way to make us perform at our best was to scare us into doing so. This is a technique often used in sport, but its success relies on the recipient being motivated and not discouraged in stressful situations. I've heard it argued that sporting competition is a stressful situation and so a coaching strategy that helps emulate the stress of the sporting performance is an effective way to get athletes fired up, but that relies on two assumptions: 1) that the athlete reacts with a fight response to attack and not a flight or freeze one, and 2) that starting from a place of high stress and managing those feelings in order to perform is more effective than starting from a place of deep calm and self-assurance. I know now that I am the latter personality type and so I had to block out a lot of mainstream noise to get myself to the 2014 Commonwealth Games.

Glasgow took the opportunity to put on this international sporting event in its stride. The east end of the city had been chronically neglected over the years with heavy industry based there and housing estates serving that industry becoming more and more dilapidated over time. Rather than exacerbate the inequalities the city was already feeling, in the years leading up to the Glasgow games, the athletes' village, cycling velodrome and cross-country mountain bike trails were all built in the city's east end in an effort to level up the disparity. Green space and cycling infrastructure now joined up what were previously concrete-bound neighbourhoods. I love that when the eyes of the world were due to turn towards Glasgow, this gritty, charming place didn't take the easy route of showcasing the already green, leafy west and south sides of the city but thought seriously about legacy and made things fairer for its residents.

The athletes' village was a huge purpose-built housing estate with entire streets dedicated to the different Commonwealth countries. Between these streets were communal areas and temporary buildings where athletes and support staff could get food, drink, entertainment and medical attention twenty-four hours a day. For two whole weeks this place buzzed and hummed with the amassed energy of hundreds of excited, nervous athletes. Moving around it felt dreamlike. Sitting on the green surrounded by some of the finest sportspeople in the world was such a privilege. Outside, the city was bouncing in anticipation and sweltering in uncharacteristically hot, sunny weather. But I couldn't enjoy any of it. I felt overwhelmed by performance anxiety and uncomfortable with the attention and care being offered by the support staff. The only time my nerves stopped jangling was when I was turning the pedals of my bike. I sat on static trainers in the athletes' village when I wasn't out on course practising or on easy spins around the city with the road riders. My event was a week into the two-week schedule and for that whole first week I would lie awake in my single bed in the cyclists' house on Scotland Street and think about all the things that could go wrong. I wasn't hungry, which was just as well as I was on a strict diet made up of one level serving spoon of rice with vegetables three times a day. There were buffet tables groaning with tasty food from all over the world and available at all hours of the day, but I couldn't eat any of it.

The line between fear and excitement is a hazy place. Physiologically, fear and excitement are effectively the same thing. Stress hormones like cortisol and adrenaline cause blood pressure and heart rate to increase. Decision-making is affected. Nausea and chest or stomach pain may follow depending on an individual's perception of the threat. From this description it's little wonder many people shy away from challenge, but the moment that pressure has somewhere to go the release is like no other feeling on earth.

The morning of the women's cross-country mountain bike race dawned fine and dry. Some of my English contemporaries opted for a lift up to the warm-up pens at the top of Cathkin Braes, but I chose to ride up there carrying my own bottles and equipment to help settle my body and mind. I tried to convince myself that this was just a race like any other and that I'd been here hundreds of times before. This was made difficult when I had to weave my way through gridlocked vehicles as I neared the Braes and then had to put my bag, bike and helmet through strict security measures to access the venue. I tried to just breathe, but my heart and head were pounding and then my vision started closing in. I needed some perspective. Just then, a familiar face appeared. My dear friend Penny was a volunteer at the games and had requested to be at the mountain bike event. Seeing her smiling, familiar face transported me back to my real life, which I was reminded would be there when all of this was over. Her kind words of reassurance brought me back to myself and helped me realise that whatever happened, the people who loved me and the life I had built would all be there to enjoy at the end of this day, regardless of the outcome.

I followed the remaining race prep steps that I had written, as always, on a tiny piece of paper tucked into my shorts leg.

9.30 Arrive, give bike to mechanic, sign on.

10 Mark bottles, check timing chip, sit.

10.20 Two minutes increasing efforts and five minutes cool-down.

10.40 Finish warm-up, change shirt.

10.45 Toilet.

10.50 Pens to start.

11 Race.

I remember the noise. I remember the pain. I remember the heat. I remember the occasional familiar face. I remember a vague sense that I was having the race of my life. I remember the devastation on realising on the penultimate lap that I had a flat rear tyre. I remember pulling into the pits and watching the jerseys of a New Zealand and English rider fly by. I remember the mechanic shouting over the roar of the crowd that my tyre wasn't flat, just soft, and to get back on and chase. I remember the surge of adrenaline that got me back on to the wheel of the New Zealand rider on the final climb and crossing the line in seventh place, looking at the back of the fifth-place rider who was within touching distance. Then I remember Ferga and family. Kind, loving, smiling faces, huge hugs and a melting away of all the anxiety that had kept my emotions locked up for so long. I wasn't disappointed. I could have placed higher, but I had ridden well and to the very edges of my ability and skill. I felt utterly satisfied with that. I also felt absolutely, one hundred per cent finished with cross-country mountain bike racing.

After an hour of smiling so hard that my cheeks threatened to go into the same level of cramp my thighs were experiencing, I rode back down the hill to the athletes' village. Some of Team Scotland had been watching on the big screen and I arrived to hugs of congratulations. I went inside for a shower and ceremoniously dropped my heart rate monitor into the bin in the bathroom.

It was the first day of the rest of my life.

'*C'est une folie! Mais c'est une belle folie,*' said the girl as she stared down at us in wonder from her vantage point on the hiking trail above us. She was right. Pushing, shoving, carrying and, occasionally, riding our bikes over some of the French Alps' most rugged off-road cols was a kind of beautiful madness.

The Grande Randonée 5 (the GR5) is a high-level walking route through the French Alps, 420 miles long and covering 30,000 metres of ascent between Geneva in the north and Nice on the Mediterranean coast. The Commonwealth Games had been my final cross-country mountain bike race and the biggest high of my life. Now, with the games behind me and my daily focus gone, I began really struggling emotionally. I felt lost and listless and was spending my days drifting about my home in Inverness unable to put my clothes in the washing machine or make eye contact with my long-suffering partner. A darkness that I didn't recognise had wrapped itself around me; I couldn't taste, see or feel anything. Joy and colour were gone. I was grieving.

Then a job opportunity with the bike company Specialized hauled me out of my depression. Vague memories of the happiness I had felt on my first cycle tour back home from Andorra had been reignited by a visit from a Warm Showers guest. The Warm Showers website is dedicated to connecting people travelling by bike with willing hosts. Ferga had signed us up, which meant Whitney from Montana had found us on their tour around the Highlands of Scotland. We gave Whitney a bed for the night and a spare tyre from the back of our bike shed and in return they gave us their friendship and an introduction to Specialized's Seek and Enjoy programme. Specialized US was looking for bike adventurers to ride its bikes, then tell their stories from all over the world. It would provide the bikes and the online platform. The rest was up to me.

I'd always considered a fat bike to be a gimmick. Another tactic by the bike industry to sell us yet more componentry that would be incompatible with the other bikes already taking up space in our sheds, but I think in this instance I was wrong.

Moses, my Specialized Fatboy, was so called due to his ability to part the waters with his massive tyres and lightweight frame. He could ride up and down steep, loose or muddy surfaces like a tractor. What's more, he made people smile and want to interact in the way walking a puppy in the park might. I could not have anticipated how many people Moses and I would affect along the GR5. Gradually, the trip became as much about the people this unusual-looking bike seemed to affect as it did about our ride, and we began documenting people's reactions to it.

Look! Some girls riding their bikes on the GR5 and one of them on … what is that? *C'est une moto?* Eh? No, a fat bike actually. It's good on gravel, snow and sand. No, it's not too heavy. Yes, it does look pretty amazing. Nope. No battery or engine. It weighs about twenty-five kilos with the bags fully loaded. Sometimes I have to carry it, yes. Yes, that bit is hard. No. No men with us. Scared? Eh? No, should we be? I started in Geneva. It's going to take about two weeks to reach Nice. Only a bit bonkers. Thank you. Thanks a lot. *Bon courage* to you too. *Au revoir*.

I began the ride alone in Thonon on the shores of Lake Geneva, but things didn't get off to an auspicious start. After a steady six-mile road spin from the water's edge, I was soon carrying my bike and for two days I negotiated steep, rough, mostly unrideable terrain, lightning storms, electric fences, a lot of mud and poor trail markings. I got rained off the route twice and was forced to sleep in cow sheds and eat old bread. More than once I found myself longing for my old life where a predictable three-hour training ride would end with a hot shower and a comfortable bed. I still have these moments on hard multi-day rides. Long periods of emotionally downward spiralling will fill me with frustration and self-doubt and I'll find myself wondering on a loop what it is I am seeking by putting myself through such hardship. Sometimes it's possible to talk myself out of these downward trajectories, but more often than not, it's exchanges with other people that give me back my perspective and help me shift my mood. I used to be adamant that an adventure like the GR5 wouldn't be pure and fulfilling if I didn't complete it alone, but, like most of my firmly held beliefs, this one has been moderated over time.

After a few days of tussling I eventually popped out in the Chamonix valley where the sun had come out, the trails had dried up and waiting there to ride with me were Jenny Graham and Ferga. The tone changed immediately. The camaraderie and warmth made everything possible again and soon we were climbing together out of the valley to the south. I find it very satisfying to overcome challenges alone, but sometimes leaning into good friends and sharing the experience feels richer.

Gaining the col out of the Chamonix valley felt easy and harmonious after my torturous solo stint, but it lulled us all into a false sense of security. The following day began easily enough, but soon the three of us were grunting, swearing, pushing and carrying our way up to 2,100 metres, and, as a reward for all our graft, the cloud level dropped and we became engulfed in a saturating, cold rain. There was a moment, I will admit now, when I thought we weren't going to make it to Nice. And then, like every time I've hit an emotional trough on an adventure, there followed a massive life-affirming high. After teetering our way over granite slabs and waterfalls with bikes balanced precariously on our backs, we made it to the refuge on the Col de la Croix du Bonhomme that marked our descent. It was still raining hard, so we joined all the other cold, wet mountain users in the warm, dry refuge and consumed our combined body weight in cake. As we sat there people glanced over whispering in our direction.

'*Les filles traversent le GR5 en vélo.*'

'*Bravo. Bon courage.*'

'*Incroyable!*'

I'm not sure it was that incredible, but it was lovely they all thought so.

When two hours had passed and the cloud had still not lifted, it was to rounds of applause and back claps of admiration that we donned our wet kit again and headed down the other side of the col on the sweetest piece of smooth singletrack imaginable. It was an afternoon I'll not forget in a long time.

Now in the beautiful Beaufort region of the Alps and with the weather breaking into wisps of non-threatening white cloud, we continued our journey south on well-marked, narrow, traversing singletrack that became steeper and steeper until we were whooping and hollering our way into the valley far below. At one point on this quality descent we learned another valuable lesson: never trust anyone's opinion who is not on a mountain bike.

'Oi [in French], it is not possible to take a bike on that route,' yelled a dog walker on the gravel road below us. 'It is too dangerous. You must come down here.'

We thanked the man and continued on our way, appreciating the full delights of the wonderful narrow and deserted trail which ran all the way down the hillside to Landry. Here, while consuming a kilo of fried potatoes and a roast chicken each from an evening market, we smiled at one another in carb-infused satisfaction and in the dawning realisation that we might actually make it to Nice after all.

The French National Parks Authority isn't a natural enabler. That is to say: No Dogs, No Camping, No Loitering, No Walking Poles (really), No Fun and definitely No Bikes. I appreciate its wish to preserve the environmentally sensitive high alpine regions of the mountains, but some of the rules just seem a bit arbitrary and to be aimed at completely deflating the enth0usiasm of anyone wanting to appreciate such environments. To travel this route on bikes requires an environmental sensitivity and a healthy respect for the mountains. We were already making frequent judgement calls on when to ride and when to walk so as not to damage the well-maintained paths or upset any walkers. Nevertheless, out of respect, we got off our bikes and pushed until we had crossed the park border again, then dropped down to Tignes on purpose-built mountain bike trails on our laden short-travel bikes, passing confused boys in full-face helmets and body armour.

The following day we pushed/rode up the Col de l'Iseran in full view of the road meandering tantalisingly close by, causing us all to wonder what it was we were striving to achieve by making life so unnecessarily hard for ourselves. It's a question I come back to often, but now, unlike then, I have an answer. I've realised that the easiest, fastest, most economical way to do things often leaves me feeling a bit empty and joyless. It may be why I make a better mountain biker than a road rider. I have always needed something to push against: a steep gradient, a poor surface, bad weather, a difference of opinion. It makes me engage the pathways in my brain that eventually lead to satisfaction and gratitude.

We ate *pain au lait* and sardines while propped against the wall of a supermarket that afternoon. Jenny and I have spent many contented hours sitting on hot tarmac in supermarket car parks and garage forecourts all over Europe. These are the natural feeding grounds of the journeying cyclist and weirdly difficult places to leave. After a good two hours in the shade eating and drinking and packing down food into our bags for the onward journey, we began chasing the setting sun upwards out of the valley towards the Col de la Vallée Etroite into an alpine fairy tale where the riding is sublime. Smooth, sandy singletrack from the magnificent col levelled out in a pristine grassy bowl where we pitched our tents and cooked dinner while the sky turned a dark green–blue.

The three of us fell into a daily rhythm of sleeping high, waking, packing down camp and eating breakfast number one then descending to the valley for breakfast number two and to stock up on lunch and dinner supplies. Often we would get stuck in the valley floor distracted by coffee, paralysed by the heat of the sun and reluctant to begin the grunt back up the next col. Each day we repeated this pattern and little by little we inched our way south.

Sometimes we got lucky and found that there were gravel roads partway up high passes. Other times we had to push or carry from the valley floor, but more often than not we found the way off the other side of the hill was bizarrely rideable. Flowing, beautifully contouring singletrack invariably gave way to something more technical on reaching the treeline, but we would always arrive in the valley floor either grinning because of the sublime riding or because we had survived it.

Most memorable was a night spent on top of the Col du Fromage near Briançon. While we were watching a lightning storm to the west and basking in the dazzling evening sunshine from the east, the mountains became just layers of varying shades of steel-blue light running as far as the eye could see, starkly revealing the distance we had either traversed or were about to. In the morning, we negotiated the tight switchbacks down to the town of Ceillac for the, by now, essential breakfast number two and reflected on our luck at being alive and in this place.

On day eleven we descended to Larche, the hot, deserted gateway to the Mercantour National Park. It was here that two policemen barred our way with arms crossed at the entrance to the park. No amount of appealing or negotiating would have persuaded them to let us pass on the GR5, even if we promised to push our bikes.

'It is not possible.'

We were used to hearing this and pressing on regardless, but not this time. While I understand and even admire the French National Park Authority's commitment to the preservation of its wild and natural places, I feel strongly that we need to facilitate people's access to them so that more people can develop a love and appreciation for such places. It's only when we love and appreciate a place that we want to protect it. I've had many heated debates on this subject and truly empathise with people who want to restrict access to a place from those who will not treat the natural world with respect, but I struggle with the absoluteness of this view. What social inequalities do we exacerbate by granting access only to those who have had the privilege of education on how to behave in the outdoors and not to others? Being told we are not allowed to go somewhere because we can't be trusted to protect it and being instead subjected to a barrage of seemingly arbitrary, patronising rules doesn't help develop a new national park-goer's affinity for a place. I would love it if the cost of the signs telling us what not to do and of policing the park was instead spent on the education of possible visitors so that they understand why they are not to do the things that cause damage. E-bikes are a fantastic tool to facilitate more people being more active more often, and limiting people's access to wild places by placing a blanket ban on them feels like a missed opportunity to engage and nurture more people's sense of being stewards of our outdoor environments that belong to no one and all of us.

But on this day our only option was to drop 1,000 metres on the road, then tackle a 2,800-metre pass, the highest in Europe, to bypass the park and get back en route. At this point, I might have said a bad word.

We found our separate rhythms and made steady progress up towards the high col in the cool of the evening, each of us working to let go of the frustration and stress of the day. The problem hadn't been the French National Park Authority. The problem had been our fixed expectation of how our day was going to play out, and when it hadn't, our inability to let go and adapt to a new plan. Then, as if to help our poor, mortal, tortured souls, a divine intervention appeared in a high alpine bowl at 2,000 metres in the middle of absolutely nowhere. We happened upon a small music festival. The pink sky hung on the shoulders of the rocky crags at the back of the lush, green bowl. Fire pits blazed and the cooking smoke from food stalls travelled straight up in the shelter of the hill behind. From our vantage point on the road we watched colourful figures moving about: some dancing, others juggling, children wrestling with limbs indistinguishable from those of the dogs they played with. Music wafted upwards to meet us, a deep, soulful beat below a clear, sharp melody held steady by a strong female voice. We glanced at each other before wordlessly making our way down to join the many tents already nestled into the base of the hillside. We put up our tent and hung our wet clothes over our bikes near a fire pit, moving around each other in the efficient way only time-tested travelling companions can. Then people started falling from the sky. A hot air balloon and light aircraft appeared, and from both, brightly coloured bodies in wing suits drifted serenely into the centre of the small festival. Aerial acrobats, the Flying Frenchies, were joining the party. We didn't waste any time getting involved ourselves and soon we were enjoying the music and the all-you-can-eat-and-drink buffet under the stars. This surreal and wonderfully transformative experience had turned what had been the worst day of the trip into one of the best.

We were glad we paused to enjoy that evening when we did because the quality of the remaining days of riding steadily deteriorated. We got sulkier and sweatier as we dropped out of the high Alps on chossy, loose limestone interspersed with an occasional blissful ribbon of dirt through old oak woodland. The GR5 meanders torturously at this point, and although we could see the sea for two whole days it didn't appear to be getting any closer until suddenly we were there and it was over and we were bereft.

We sat on the busy beach in the fading sun and tried to adjust to our ending. Ferga helpfully reminded me that I had said I would ride Moses into the sea if we reached Nice, and so I did. My beloved fat bike has never been the same since, but it was a fitting end to one of the most challenging and rewarding adventures of my life so far. Moses and I floated. A beautiful madness. *Une belle folie.*

CHAPTER 7
THE ADVENTURE SYNDICATE

The world of competitive mountain bike racing is very far removed from the reasons I began riding a bike in the first place. The arbitrary nature of racing itself and the all-consuming training that must take place before you even reach the start line make it all so unlikely that I stuck at it for so long in the first place. Uglier still is what goes on behind the scenes. Here, an entire world of industry and politics exists that conspires to turn the sport into a business. When I was racing full-time, there was not much money in cross-country mountain biking (practically none when compared with road racing, for example), but the motivation for the brands I represented seemed to be the same. Bike and apparel manufacturers had profit margins and marketing targets like everyone else so it shouldn't have come as a surprise that these brands would only be interested in me as a commodity. What did surprise me was what my sponsors considered profitable, though. I assumed that my race results would be the most important thing to them, but I quickly understood that how I looked was of much more relevance. This didn't seem to be the case for my male counterparts. Between 2006 and 2014, the marketing departments of the bike brands I was involved with were run exclusively by white men, the majority of whom were pretty out of shape but who felt it was acceptable to pass comment on the body shapes of their female riders, and any woman for that matter. Media coverage of female bike riders showed the same shapes and skin colours displaying the range of apparel available to us in pink, purple or baby blue. The bike on which I raced at the Commonwealth Games was three inches too big for me because Cannondale didn't produce their race-specific Flash 29er in anything smaller. Things might have been different if I had been a world champion, but despite being one of the best riders in the UK, I was a small-hitter on the international circuit and being seen was more important than performing well.

I had come full circle. Fitting in and looking the part had become my livelihood. This irony wasn't lost on my thirteen-year-old self.

The world has changed considerably since then thanks to the Black Lives Matter and #MeToo movements, but in many ways all that has happened is that the inequalities in our society have been brought out of the shadows. The work to address them remains to be done.

While it never sat comfortably with me that some people received support and others didn't, depending on the whims of a privileged few in marketing departments, I am eternally grateful for the support I received from bike brands and from Scottish Cycling and British Cycling. There were some real gems of individuals who did all they could to support and encourage me behind the scenes while having to meet brutal, inhumane targets to justify their decisions. I suspect that the changes now taking place in the competitive cycling world are largely down to the efforts of these excellent people who gently challenged chauvinistic, racist and homophobic systems from the inside. They were ahead of their time in their recognition that cycling could be used to reduce inequalities. I made myself promise that as soon as I no longer needed sponsorship and selection to reach Glasgow 2014, I'd do my bit to redress the dearth of diversity that existed then in the adventure sports world.

The Adventure Syndicate was my attempt to do that. In the summer of 2015, I visited the home of prominent blogger, cycle courier and round-the-world bike rider, Emily Chappell, in London. Together we planned to join the masses of people riding the Dunwich Dynamo, a 100-mile ride that departs at 10 p.m. from

London Fields and arrives on the Norfolk coast for sunrise the following day. The ride starts on a Saturday night, and so we thought we should stay up all night on Friday so we would sleep the following day in preparation for our night shift. What we didn't account for was that we'd have so much to talk about we'd end up staying awake for forty-eight hours. It was under these sleep-deprived, adrenaline-fuelled conditions and the buoyancy that comes from meeting a kindred spirit that The Adventure Syndicate was born. Emily and I shared a passion for offering the bike industry and the sporting world an alternative narrative that was more repre-sentative of a cross-section of society. Our idea was to establish a collective of extraordinary women, well known in the niche world of adventure but whose voices were not heard in mainstream media. We would not make our gender a focal point but leave this fact up to our audience to interpret however they chose. We talked long and hard about the pros and cons of The Adventure Syndicate being female-only and settled on it being female or non-binary led. If what we were doing spoke to someone, we wanted them, regardless of gender, to feel part of an alternative narrative to that of the solo conquering hero; a narrative that promoted the strength and power of collective, collaborative grace. I should say that this was not what we both embodied by the end of the Dunwich Dynamo weekend. Emily and I were husks of our former selves, completely wrung out and weepy with exhaustion but with a shared excitement bubbling somewhere deep below the surface that we both knew would blossom into something pretty exciting.

By the following spring, we had recovered enough from the Dunwich Dynamo to commit to our first challenge together. We'd spent the winter reaching out to shared contacts in the bike industry and adventure cycling world to establish our own brand that we hoped would provide an inspiring and encouraging alternative to being physical in the mainstream media.

Mark Beaumont had just set a record for riding a recently estab-lished 500-mile road route around the north-west Highlands of Scot-land non-stop. So to launch The Adventure Syndicate, Emily and I gathered a team around us and set about preparing to break Mark's record. We wanted to show what groups of strong, enduring, cooperative, caring people could achieve together in a sporting context where aggression, strength and speed usually dominate. Our all-female non-stop team time trial around the North Coast 500 was our attempt to do just that.

I'll admit now I had no idea of the can of worms I was opening when I began organising that challenge. The logistics involved in keeping seven women and their bikes on the move using a support crew of eight are mind-boggling. Chuck into that a call to action to encourage other people to join us along the way and the commissioning of a film crew to document the journey and my brain was at full capacity. I had to get someone else to remind me to swallow and blink during the first two weeks of May. Emily took charge of social media leaving me free to plan on-the-ground logistics, but with food, vehicles, crew, roles, tactics, equipment, strategy, contingency, journalists, kit donations, SPOT trackers, pre-ride accommodation and film narratives still to consider, it's little wonder that the night before the ride began, my bike was still in bits and I couldn't find any shorts to wear.

Fortunately, The Adventure Syndicate had managed to recruit the most incredible team of experienced self-sufficient riders and creative, hard-working support crew imaginable.

We assembled at my home in Inverness the Thursday evening before our scheduled 6 a.m. Saturday departure to go over my fastidiously compiled eight-page document that detailed the roles and responsibilities of each rider and support crew member. Our goal was to get at least one rider round the entire 518 miles non-stop in thirty-six hours. Rickie Cotter (British twenty-four-hour MTB champ), Joanne Thom and Zara Mair (Pedal Power's endurance and adventure racing female pair), and Emily Chappell (transcontinental racer and ultra-endurance cyclist) were put in the positions of protected riders. It was everyone else's job to ensure these riders remained shielded from the wind at all times, had to make minimal decisions, were kept fuelled and hydrated and, at 4 a.m. when conversation would inevitably dry up, entertained with games and songs. In support of these four was a star cast of experienced bunch riders. Gaby Leveridge (Starley pro cyclist) and Anne Ewing (my Team Scotland ally in the 2014 Commonwealth Games) would assist me in organising the group as they rode, ensuring lead riders never had to take a turn on the front, going back to the vehicles for food, water or clothing, and making sure that radio contact was maintained with the support crew throughout the night. Anne, in typical style, would arrive at 6 a.m. on Saturday still brushing her teeth straight off her shift as a doctor in the central belt.

Back before The Adventure Syndicate began properly considering the environmental cost of its endeavours, we thought nothing of recruiting three teams in three vehicles to support our attempt. The film crew and friends Kirk and Lindsay would be driven in vehicle one by riding buddy David Jones to set up shots and take drone footage of the riders. Little did they know their camera equipment would soon be mixed in with our chamois cream and spare wheels, and that we would commandeer their driver to ride with us when we needed fresh conversation. Team Life Support would be driven in vehicle two by members of the Torridon Mountain Rescue Team, Gordy and Tom, while our head of communications, Jenny Graham (who at the time was an inexperienced road rider but who now needs no introduction as the fastest woman to ride around the world), and our head of catering, Laura, would work tirelessly in the back of the vehicle to organise our regular and ever more random food requests. (In the end Laura and Jenny took to just asking, 'Sweet or savoury?', and something would appear out of the window that could have been either.) In the third and final vehicle was Team Bike Preservation, consisting of Pete and Fraser, whose job it was to keep bikes on the road and draft support riders back to the main bunch after pee stops or punctures.

It was with a mixture of relief and anticipation that we all eventually rolled out of Inverness at 6 a.m. on Saturday 14 May and started making our steady way west towards brightening skies. We whipped along as one big group, all politely not mentioning the significant sidewind that we knew would be in our faces when we reached the sea at Applecross and turned north. Having agreed to a stopping strategy of five minutes every four hours to pee and refuel,

I pulled my first mean trick of the ride by announcing there would be no scheduled stop until we had descended off the Bealach na Bà, after five hours of riding. This definitely was not in keeping with the cooperation and collaboration theme, but knowing the characters on this ride well, I knew they would let any pressing needs be known and that they all understood that the focus had to be on the group and not on individual needs.

The climb up the formidable Bealach na Bà was a bit too fast to be sustainable over a thirty-six-hour period, but everyone was still so fresh and enjoying themselves so much that it seemed a shame to rein in their enthusiasm. We topped out all together under a now cloudless sky and sailed down to the blindingly blue sea. It was a wonderful feeling, descending at speeds of up to forty miles per hour in the company of these women on this classic road, each of us utterly at ease and trusting of the fast, perfect line being taken in front of us. A five-minute resupply and pee stop while Gordy shouted out time checks and Peter and Fraser fiddled with my slipping gears, then Gaby and Anne peeled off to rest up for their later efforts. The five remaining riders then turned north into a headwind and began pressing on round the rolling coast to Shieldaig.

As the Isle of Skye gradually slipped out of our peripheral vision, we wiggled our way up and over the coast road and into Glen Torridon where we enjoyed a brief respite from the wind while riding up the sheltered glen before swinging north-west again along Loch Maree. By this time Team Life Support had picked up Tom from his home in Torridon and the radio evidence suggested they were having quite a nice time in the van. All the way up the relentless hill out of Dundonnell, they played us an unusual mix of what I think was supposed to be motivational music through the radio in my jersey pocket. Had we had the breath and the inclination we might have joined in their singing.

On the long descent into Ullapool from the Braemore junction I knew I had to make a judgement call. I'd ridden 200 miles in support of our four lead riders and if I were to be of any use to them later in the ride I had to rest. I had a brief battle with my ego before giving myself a good talking to. The plan had always been to maximise our chances of getting one rider round the entire route non-stop in the fastest time possible. My staying on the bike now would not help achieve that collective goal and would only give the remaining support riders more lead riders to protect during the dark hours that were to follow. I had a brief check-in with the four remaining riders who all expressed their keenness to carry on, before climbing off my bike in a bit of a grump in Ullapool. My grump was short-lived. Anne got back on her bike and I jumped into the campervan with Kirk and Lindsay after a dinner of fish and chips and good chat by the sea. We were a full hour ahead of schedule.

Forty minutes later I woke with a start. BANG.

'There's been a crash. Shit! There's been a crash.'

I jumped out of the van (remembering just in time to zip my drop-seat shorts back up) to find all the riders in a heap on the tarmac just south of the Ledmore junction.

'What happened, Anne?'

'I don't know … a touch of wheels … Rickie went down … Em went over her.'

The other riders all got to their feet, but Emily stayed on the ground, in obvious shock with the pain she was experiencing in both knees. Eventually she recovered enough to communicate that she was okay, and the other riders and support vehicles got back on the road. We lifted Em into the campervan where we discovered that the medicinal properties of cold chips work wonders on badly bruised knees and dented morale. We swaddled Em in down sleeping bags and tucked her up for the night. A rider as strong as her would prove useful to the team in the morning if we could help her rest and recover enough to get back on her bike once it got light again.

The remaining team rolled on into the evening round the Lochinver coastal road, led by Anne in the gathering darkness. Anne's ability to keep tired, disorganised riders together is second to none and all through the evening, while the rain tapped on the campervan windscreen, Jenny and I communicated with Anne, and Anne with our remaining lead riders Rickie, Jo and Zara. Gaby, meanwhile, had been recruited to drive Team Bike Preservation's van while Pete got some sleep. This was the strength in depth of our team. A professional rider with the skill and experience of Gaby Leveridge was mucking in with whatever needed to be done to achieve our collective goal.

At midnight, I got back out on my bike. This was my watch: the witching hours. With 280 miles done and 230 left to go the last thing anyone wants is to feel the air get colder, the darkness even darker and the night stretching out ahead for an unfathomably long time, but I knew that if we got Rickie, Jo and Zara through this period on schedule we stood a good chance of achieving our goal: one rider round the North Coast 500 in under thirty-six hours.

The four of us turned east and crept on through the night. Although it was getting hard for the riders who had not stopped at all, spirits seemed pretty high after our five-minute 1 a.m. coffee stop. Our four lights bobbed about in the darkness while up ahead the tail lights of the Life Support vehicle gave us something to focus our drooping eyelids on. At some point we became aware of a strong, silent presence behind us. Fraser had hopped out of the Bike Preservation vehicle and was tailing us like a guardian angel. He and I rode together at the front for a while, reminiscing over the shortest day of the previous year when something close to insanity had inspired a group of us to ride on frozen roads from Thurso to Lairg. The Suicide Ride, as we affectionately remember it, was a sobering lesson in the vulnerability of the human body. The temperature had dropped so sharply when the sun went down that it turned our sodden clothing and the damp tarmac to ice. When I pulled over to put another layer on, my cold fingers wouldn't comply with zippers and clips. I got back on my bike and attempted to ride faster to warm up, but the black ice on the road made it impossible. We all survived that one, but it made us think long and hard about just how quickly things could go wrong.

Six months later and back on the North Coast 500 it was 4 a.m. and Rickie and I had broken into Nina Simone's 'Feeling Good' as daylight gradually made itself known near Tongue. This is the best part of riding through the night for me. The impending doom felt just a few hours previously gives way to euphoria when the night begins to evaporate; when that feeling of having survived something against the odds emerges. Riding through the night fills me with a deep, life-affirming satisfaction and my capacity for enduring hard things expands each time I do it.

The four of us marvelled as seeping light revealed the steep, rocky coastline into which we had heard the mighty sea crash all night. Then at around 5 a.m., Gordy pulled a van alongside us and Jenny's tired but still smiling face appeared.

'It's Harriet Pike on the phone. The SPOT tracker needs a reset.'

Our friends in Bristol had stayed up all night watching our GPS unit inch its way around the coast. We reset the tracker and sang our thanks to Harriet on the other end of the phone. Out here on the road our challenge was already a huge team effort, but this was a reminder that our team extended far beyond the people within eyeshot. It was so often this way in my more formal racing days too. I often felt somehow that a collective energy was behind me and willing me on, without being able to name specific people who might be contributing. In years to come, my friend Sarah Outen would describe this feeling as having an 'invisible peloton' alongside her on adventures, sheltering her from the wind and providing comfort and camaraderie.

Rickie remained solid throughout the night. When I dreamt this team up, Rickie immediately sprang to mind. This wee Welsh rocket has an incredible capacity to manage pain and discomfort, and her sense of humour, insight and understanding makes most people warm to her instantly. Two years later, Rickie and I would ride the Tour Divide together, a 2,745-mile self-supported non-stop mountain bike time trial from Canada to Mexico. I would nearly die and Rickie would be disqualified, but we'd make an entirely self-shot film of our adventure that would win awards and hearts all over the world. We didn't know any of that then.

Together Jo and Zara made a phenomenal team. They had raced together so much that they instinctively knew how to check in with each other to ensure they were eating and drinking enough and still operating their bikes safely. But while Rickie chirped away and I had to constantly tell her to get off the front and save energy by hanging on to my wheel, Jo and Zara went into a dark place. It was interesting to see how they both handled this. Jo, with her extensive experience of suffering like this, made clear demands ('I need you to talk to me.' 'Can we play a game?' 'Come on, Jo!'). Whereas Zara slipped further into the physical pain of her rebelling stomach.

From the back seat of Team Life Support, Jenny calculated that our average speed had dropped so much that we were now thirty minutes behind our target. I took a risk by suggesting we speed up by two miles per hour in the hope this would change Jo and Zara's emotional gear. This would be kill or cure for Zara. She told me afterwards just how close she was to getting in that van right then, but as the hills gradually gave way to flatter terrain ('I don't much like your hill, Betty,' Rickie bellowed as we hauled ourselves through Bettyhill), Zara got back into her groove, showing incredible willpower, while Jo remained in her dark place almost to the end of the ride. This is impressive in itself. To carry on for seventeen hours after first feeling down is tenacious in the extreme.

One by one riders woke up and got back on their bikes until we found ourselves ten-strong having picked up some supporters along the way. We wheeled round John o'Groats before turning south at 10 a.m. It now didn't matter what state I got myself into. With so many strong, rested, experienced riders ready to take their turn in supporting Rickie, Jo and Zara home, I decided to stay on my bike all the way to Inverness.

We now had 'just' 120 miles to ride and we were home and dry. But the A9 is a horrible road to ride on: busy and steep in sections, with a vicious westerly wind that whips off the flat moorland and races to the sea. It was time for my darkest hour. The world twisted so that the road didn't look real and I observed with removed interest how my body seemed to be refusing to do the simple things I asked it to. Now tucked away from the headwind while Gaby and a much-recovered Emily towed us south, aided by female support riders from Wick Wheelers and Thurso, I continued to keep a watchful eye on Rickie, Jo and Zara – but now instead of shielding them from the sidewind I blatantly ordered other people to. This was proving a nice little plan, and I tucked my tired body in behind Rickie so I could keep half an eye on her body language. Until she puked on me. It's a thankless task being a support rider.

We were back on schedule, but our bodies were beginning to rebel. Our toilet breaks were becoming more frequent, and we were constantly back and forth between vans as we tried to fuel our systems with anything we thought we could keep down. Golspie, Tain, Alness: we were now in familiar territory, but we still had to hold it together for the final push. The riding was getting ragged and we were losing momentum.

I got on the radio to work out our timings.

'Lee to Laura?'

Laura's voice crackled back in answer. She had abandoned her sticky catering unit, which now more resembled a crime scene, and was working frantically on our timings. We had sixty minutes to cover the remaining twenty-three miles into Inverness if we wanted to hit our thirty-six-hour target. This wouldn't have been so hard on a normal Sunday run, but we had hundreds of miles in our legs and had had little or no sleep. We were averaging twelve miles per hour. With a massive team effort we raised the pace through Beauly and tried to organise ourselves into an efficient peloton. There were some very experienced riders in the group but no one person calling the shots, and with adrenaline running high now, things were starting to blow apart. Rickie was shouting for someone, anyone, to lead her out, and for a moment it looked as though she was going to be towed away from Jo and Zara to end up back in Inverness a solo victorious rider. Somehow, above all the crosswinds and frantic panic and ragged riding, Gaby, Anne and I ordered the remaining seven riders into a through-and-off formation (like that seen in professional team time trials but with more soiled clothing and bloodied knees). Together with Jenny, Paula and Fraser we managed to regain control of the rabble on bikes and pinned the remaining eight miles into town at speeds of nearly thirty miles per hour. As we approached the city limits, somewhere in my tired brain I found the strength to take charge as the group started to fall apart again.

'Rickie! Remember what we are doing this for! We finish together. And alive!'

She backed off the pace, stopped at the red light at Clachnaharry and allowed everyone to regroup.

All seven riders finished the ride together in thirty-six hours and thirty seconds, a new record. I happily concede those thirty seconds to finishing as a group having all worked so tirelessly to achieve our joint aim.

Looking back, I can't quite believe we pulled it off. I am constantly surprised by what it is possible to achieve when a group of people share a common goal, compassion for each other and a willingness to cooperate, compromise and dig that bit deeper when the going gets really tough. The glow I was left with from that ride emanated from the spirit under which the challenge was taken up and executed. Every single member of our team was required to make sure we achieved our aim on the North Coast 500 and it's so fitting that The Adventure Syndicate began on those foundations.

Emily would eventually step down from The Adventure Syndicate and Jenny Graham would step up. Jenny would bring with her the energy and insight that makes her the excellent rider, youth worker, adventure buddy and friend that she is. Our not-for-profit organisation would go on to take groups of teenage girls on overnight bikepacking trips into the hills, run training camps and events to bring like-minded women together and hatch adventure plans of their own, race solo and in teams all over the world and, most importantly, tell the stories of these adventures in engaging, accessible ways. Our North Coast 500 team time trial record attempt was the start of The Adventure Syndicate's mission to rewrite the Hero's Journey narrative. Stories involving brave men breaking records and pushing limits, then returning home with wisdom and insights to share have been told for centuries. They invoke awe and admiration while also maintaining a distance between protagonist and audience. But by taking on challenges governed by a set of values that include care, compassion and collaboration, shifting the emphasis of these stories to the 'how' and not simply the 'what', we can turn them from entertaining folklore into the possible inspiration for a diverse new generation hooked on meaningful adventure.

CHAPTER 8
THE TRANS PYRENEES

I first met Durita Holm ten years ago in Granada, while escaping the Scottish winter. A mountain bike guiding company run by two dear friends in the Spanish Sierra Nevada mountains employed us both as guides. Shaun and Csilla of Ride Sierra Nevada let me pitch my handmade yurt amongst the cherry trees on their *campo* and each winter I would migrate south with the birds from the Highlands of Scotland to enjoy tent life in the Spanish sunshine. During these three or four months, Durita and I would work for Shaun when required and ride together the rest of the time, following a haphazard training programme that promised to make us the Scottish and Andalusian mountain bike champions respectively. It did this, and it also made us lifelong friends, something that these days I hold far dearer than any championship title.

When she was nineteen, Durita worked for a year on a fishing boat alongside fifteen men in order to earn her share in a twenty-foot yacht that she then sailed from her home in the Faroe Islands around the world. In the first year of her three-year voyage she became pregnant, paused briefly in New Zealand to give birth, then resumed her travels with her baby daughter, eventually ending up in Spain. Now a mindfulness and meditation teacher, Durita lives in the house she built herself, surrounded by horses and dogs, on the other side of the valley from Shaun and Csilla. Despite our distance from each other and our busy lives, we always make the effort to meet up at least once a year to go on an adventure. Spending time with an old friend who shares your past and who you know will be at the centre of your future is such a nurturing thing to do. There is no pretending. We know, love and accept each other for who we are, which frees up a lot of energy. The word 'accept' in Faroese is 'gotka'. It literally means 'good take'. Where the English language suggests that to accept a person or a situation is to make do or to settle for less, the Faroese don't consider the concept of acceptance without the good – devoid of judgement of that person or situation. Acceptance in Faroese only happens when they 'take the good' of someone or something. Spending time with someone who approaches the world this way is a real gift. Because of our shared history, Durita and I are able to bypass the pleasantries and get straight on to discussing the big stuff: love, loss, spirituality, existentialism, jealousy, competitiveness. Nothing is out of bounds. These conversations have helped us as individuals and our friendship to grow over the years, and they become all the more transformative when we're on a challenging journey somewhere together in the mountains. Which is why we had decided that this autumn we should ride across the Pyrenees from west to east.

We had attempted this journey before off-road with a group of friends but had one by one been struck down by giardia and had had to abandon our ambitious itinerary halfway along the mountain range. This time our plan was to follow a road route from Saint-Jean-de-Luz on the Atlantic coast over the classic road cols made famous by the Tour de France: Col d'Aubisque, Col du Tourmalet, Col d'Aspin. Having never learned our lesson about running to tight timeframes, we would have to ride all day for six days to complete our route. We would sleep wild and grow feral and use the combined determination of two ex-mountain bike racers to haul ourselves and our kit over col after freezing col to reach Collioure on the Mediterranean coast before the weather changed for good that year.

Against all the odds, we met in San Sebastián one mid-September morning. I hadn't been to bed in thirty-six hours and in that time had squeezed in a fifty-five-mile mountain bike race back in Scotland. Durita had travelled up from the south of Spain by bus to meet me. She had brought with her a broken bike, an Ikea bag of items and a heavy cold, so it's not surprising it took us quite a lot longer than anticipated to get going that day. We ended up riding only twelve miles up the coast where we drank beer, ate pizza and slept under the watchful gaze of a lighthouse. But the following day, with renewed energy and enthusiasm (derived largely from coffee and croissants), we pored over some maps and planned our route out of town.

It quickly transpired that I was in charge. Durita had no stomach for navigation or campcraft, and happily abdicated all responsibility. I challenged her on this. Durita had sailed around the world and travelled extensively overland too.

'Yes, I did navigate around the world by boat, but all I had to do was keep going west and try to stay on the ocean.'

'Okay, okay. I just need you to remember one thing. We are looking for the D933. Can you just remember that?'

'But that's four things! I can remember the D.'

When we eventually found our road, it carried us almost imperceptibly upwards and into the soft, rolling foothills of the Pyrenees. The air was clear and crisp, and although we could tell winter was coming, we felt hopeful it would wait another week.

On our second night on the road, I was given a lesson in mindfulness. We arrived in Oloron on a scented wave of chocolate and spent a good hour sniffing our way around the town trying to find the Lindt factory that was its source. We didn't find it, which was probably for the best, but now, with the afternoon giving way to dusk, my thoughts turned to finding a spot for the tent, shopping for dinner and getting an early night in preparation for the following day of riding. But according to Durita, to do what you have always done just because you have always done it that way is life-limiting. Instead, she suggested: 'We must go to the bar.' This was a theme that was to be repeated most evenings. Durita was intent on saving my soul by encouraging me to let go of any plans and instead live in each moment. This often meant we snacked on bar food instead of dinner then slept rough just outside built-up areas, but this freedom from any kind of itinerary was intoxicating. After ten years of following strict training plans and accounting for every minute dedicated towards my end goal of becoming faster on a bike, exposure to this new way of being was exactly what I needed.

At the end of each evening's drinking, Durita would produce, with a flourish, a lightweight rucksack, into which she bundled all the things that had spilled out of her carefully packed bikepacking bags when we had sat down for the first round of beers hours before. Clothes, snacks and maps all got swept off the table and into the Too-Pissed-To-Pack Sack before being slung over one broad shoulder and carried rakishly off into the darkness.

After our second night in the corner of a field on the outskirts of town we resumed our glorified pub crawl up and over the cols d'Aubisque and Soulor. With the forecast predicting rain that would be turning to snow on high ground, we expected to see nothing of the spectacular high alpine landscape that links these two passes. This road is dubbed Little Tibet because of its desolate, wild beauty and delicate alpine tundra, but we had resigned ourselves to seeing only ten feet into the freezing, enveloping cloud that would surely surround us at such altitude. However, we somehow managed to stay a wheel ahead of the weather all day and witnessed the landscape at its most atmospheric. An entire morning spent climbing was followed by an hour of effortless descending. Effortless, unless you count the shivering. By the time we were a mile into any descent, the sweat generated on the climb had frozen to ice on our backs.

Durita stopped at the top of our second col that day and, with a sage smile, donned an entire ski outfit. Conversely, because of my sleep-deprived state when leaving Scotland, I had completely failed to pack even a set of leg warmers. Back in the winter of 2010, I had developed pneumonia while winter training with Durita in the Sierra Nevada, yet here I was again and with only myself to blame. That afternoon we arrived in the town of Argelès-Gazost, me nursing an ice cream headache from the freezing descent and whimpering quietly. Then we struck gold: a quiet spa campsite, officially closed for the winter, positioned right next to a bakery and a beer shop. Durita's eyes rolled back in her head and we put up our tent, giggling at our good fortune.

I'm not sure I believe in good fortune these days. These fortuitous experiences have happened to me too often while travelling by bike to be chance or coincidence. I've had periods of my life when everything goes right and times when one catastrophe follows another. What I understand now is that to a significant degree, how I frame an experience tends to dictate what will follow. There is a weird comfort in wallowing in disaster and negativity, but it's far more rewarding in the long run to find the good in people and situations. In the same way as a cat will make a beeline for the person in the room who dislikes cats, we attract negativity if we scowl and bad-mouth others. Conversely, by being governed by kindness and by remaining open, good things happen to us in turn. This way of being has always been easy in the company of friends like Durita.

It was hard to leave our spa site with the weather still glowering at us from the Col du Tourmalet high above. It took us the best part of the day to climb the mother of all cols, but, again, we managed to escape the pessimistic forecast and made it over the Col d'Aspin too.

Now three days into the hills, and with our kit set-up finally sorted, we were starting our days earlier and increasing our mileage steadily. Having lost half a day to the spa campsite, we were faced with needing to average sixty hilly miles a day in order to keep to our travel plans home from Barcelona the following week. If we kept riding for eight hours a day, we would take six days in total to reach the coast. But the rules adopted on day one still applied: no life-limiting planning; no sticking rigidly to an itinerary. We must remain flexible and free and always, *always* stop for beer if the opportunity arose.

We got over the Col de Peyresourde and dropped like stones past the town of Bagnères-de-Luchon to the valley below, then slammed straight into a mean headwind whipping up off the flat plains to the north. With twenty miles to complete before turning out of the wind to the east, we were passed by a fast-looking woman dressed in full Lycra on a carbon road bike. Without a word, we increased our speed until we were sitting on her wheel. With my dirty, baggy shorts flapping in the wind astride a loaded gravel bike and Durita on her ancient road bike with stuff sacks strapped to the frame and two carrots sitting proudly in a pouch on her handlebars (no gears, incidentally, as her cable outers had long since perished over time) the pair of us spent a nauseating half-hour at the mercy of our egos. Eventually we cheerily waved our new friend goodbye at a road junction then, when out of sight, pulled over and hung over our handlebars, fighting for enough oxygen to dissipate the lactic acid coursing through our bodies. I love that Durita and I still rise unquestioningly to competitive challenges. There's something very special about contentedly sipping coffee in a roadside cafe while discussing the Buddhist theory of non-permanence, then, twenty minutes later, responding unthinkingly to some primal competitive urge that has you hanging off a complete stranger's wheel. What I love more is that these days we will do it with an array of root vegetables poking out of our bar bags.

The Ariège region is the one place in the world I would consider swapping Scotland for. At its heart lies the quirky market town of Saint-Girons and for a twenty-mile radius, tiny mountain hamlets nestle into lush, green, wooded hillsides, watched over by glowering high peaks. At this time of year, the sun sits lazily in the sky, tired out by the persistence of summer, making everything slightly softer and more subtle.

We entered the region by the Col de Portet d'Aspet. This was our third big climb of the day and we were bone-tired. On arriving at the top, the delicate notes of a piano drifted towards us on the air, which we followed until we found their source: a dilapidated restaurant selling dusty jars of honey and beer from a small fridge. The hairless head of a man was bent over the piano keys in concentration and rapture while he delivered a soulful rendition of a Rachmaninov concerto. Durita and I moved spellbound into the cool, dark room and wordlessly we sat down to allow the melancholic music to sweep over us and melt away the tension in our fatigued bodies. Then, without warning, we were both in tears. There was no torment accompanying this unexpected shared sadness. It was as though the physical exertion of the day had worn the barrier between feeling and thought really thin and there was now nothing to prevent this raw beautiful sound having such an effect on us. Fatigue helps us to feel things. A sixty-mile ride over hilly terrain followed by a soulful musical rendition tapped into what Durita later explained as our 'llantos'. Translated from the Spanish this means 'teary sadness', but in a constructive, peaceful way. A person's llantos is the bodily processing of loss or grief. We didn't know what we had been carrying with us until that point on the ride, but I am sure whatever it was is always there within me. A good cry when physically depleted and exposed to beauty can feel like a really nourishing gift to yourself.

Back in the cafe at the top of a col in the Haute-Pyrénées, our pianist looked up from his keys to take in the two dirty, tear-stained cyclists, then said with a Gallic shrug:

'This is always happening.'

We moved slowly through the region, taking deep breaths and fantasising about a possible life here. We stopped for a lazy lunch in Massat amongst wild flowers and bumblebees and enjoyed the passing company of friendly local residents.

Much later than was respectable, we began our climb out of the valley up the Col de Port but made up for our lunchtime lethargy by time-trialling the only busy artery road we had encountered on the entire trip in order to make Ax-les-Thermes before nightfall. This interesting thermal spa town is cradled by a steep bowl on the border of the region and it marked the starting point of the last full, classic col we had to ride over. We bivvied in some trees 200 vertical metres above the town that night, Durita executing the final climb of the day in full ski kit and carrying the Too-Pissed-To-Pack Sack. When we awoke the following morning, it was to an impressive dawn and to the realisation that our secluded, wild patch of trees was actually the lower terrace of someone's garden.

It remained cold as we inched our way up the remainder of the north-facing 2,000-metre Port de Pailhères for the rest of that morning before topping out into late morning sunshine and a breathtaking view over layers of wooded hilltops in all their autumn glory. From here, it was mostly downhill through the Pyrénées-

Orientales to the Mediterranean coast, but the prospect of dropping out of the high mountains felt bittersweet to me. There is some satisfaction that accompanies the descent from a successful high-level mountain traverse such as this, but, especially in autumn, there is also a deep melancholy. While the leaves of deciduous trees make their spectacular exit in a burning flourish of red and gold, endings of all sorts are brought into sharp focus. For Durita and me, it meant the imminent return to our complicated lives away from the simplicity of travelling by bike and the easy company of each other. But for now, we tried to appreciate the intense beauty of these colours for what it was and not what it heralded.

It had surprised me to learn that the oranges, browns and reds of autumn that I feel so drawn to are the natural colours of the leaves. Green leaves are the tree putting on a show, a chlorophyll mask worn all summer to absorb energy from the sun. But at this time of year, they give up their exhausting task of pretending to be something they are not and reveal their glorious vulnerability and spectacular beauty for a precious short time. Since understanding that, autumn has always reminded me to relax and let go. Keeping up the highly charged intensity of the summer months is exciting but tiring. The time I spend each autumn with Durita feels like a purging of an unsustainable way of being, a letting go of tension and expectation and melting into a softer, kinder way of being for a few months. I don't sleep much in the summer and feel the repercussions of this in the winter. Autumn heralds this change of pace, and with it always seems to come grief and relief.

Eventually, a network of tiny roads filtered us into the final valley floor where we turned east before cruising downhill to the sea on a well-marked cycle track. We reached Collioure at lunchtime on 28 September and sat on the pebbled beach taking in the scene that had inspired Matisse, Picasso and Charles Rennie Mackintosh. We were striped with dirt and sunburn to a level we hadn't appreciated until we removed our cycling clothes and made for the water's edge. It felt appropriate to mark the end of our traverse as we had started: sleep deprived but functioning as a result of pizza, beer and each other's company. We slept that night on the beach under a full moon so bright it had us squinting behind our closed eyelids, but eventually we drifted off to sleep listening to the lacklustre waves trundling into the sea wall.

The following day we rode slowly down the coast to Lake Banyoles to reach our friends Gareth and Fiona at Girona Cycling, our hosts for the trip's final evening. In my racing days, the Scottish Cycling team would descend on Gareth and Fiona for weeks at a time in the winter, making use of their beautiful, spacious accommodation, their bike and fitness knowledge, their unflappable hospitality and their three-course meals. They welcomed us like family and we sat at the grand dining room table alongside the other hotel guests who were also all in the northern Pyrenees to ride bikes in the remaining warmth of the year.

That evening, we sat in the same spot on the balcony that I had often occupied after a hard day of winter training and marvelled at the passing of time. We agreed that life was, in general, more complicated these days. We were no longer two young mountain bike racers focused entirely on ourselves and our fitness, and were now heading home to resume our normal lives where decisions and responsibilities lay in wait and winter conspired to rob our energy and focus further. But for the last six days, life had taken on the simplicity and vitality of the summer of our youth. What's more, we agreed our experience had been enriched by a wisdom we didn't have back then. A net gain, we thought. We would do this again.

CHAPTER 9
THE TOUR DIVIDE –
PART ONE

My enthusiasm for travelling self-supported by bike in the mountains had grown considerably since retiring from cross-country racing. I didn't miss the constant stress and pressure of elite-level racing, but I did miss the focus and feel of the physical challenge. Now, with a community of strong, competent women in my life such as Emily Chappell, Laura Moss and Harriet Pike (the first board of directors of The Adventure Syndicate), I began entertaining the idea of getting involved in the world of long-distance, self-supported bikepacking racing. The grandmother of these races is the Tour Divide.

In my dreams of racing from Canada to Mexico on the Tour Divide, I had conjured up a heroic image of myself moving effort-lessly through majestic mountain ranges, over high plains and through hot desert; of sleeping under the stars and finding the same rhythm as all the other wild creatures who survive out there in the vast emptiness of the western United States. In reality, as is always the case, things would prove a little different.

It took me three years of daydreaming to edge my fantasy towards reality. I felt that I needed to get my head around the scale of the challenge first. I wanted to try and fully prepare myself – mind, body and equipment – to ride the 2,745 off-road miles over the equivalent height of five Mount Everests. It turned out I needn't have bothered. There was nothing that could have prepared me for riding the Tour Divide. I should have just leapt in with lower expectations sooner, but in 2017 that wasn't really my style. I was still a drilled athlete who believed on some level in the importance of meticulous preparation.

I consider now all the precision thinking that went into preparing for this ride and all the minuscule tweaks and tucks and weighing of gear that I sweated and laboured over in the months before leaving and I laugh out loud. I wonder how many potential adventures are discarded by people every day because they convince themselves they are not ready for the challenge. In reality, no one can ever be completely ready for an adventure. An adventure by definition has an unknown outcome, and it will always deliver different lessons and produce better memories to spite our expectations.

Rickie Cotter and I began the Tour Divide as two whole, clean, intact beings on finely tuned bikes all neatly packed and ordered. We finished two feral, unwashed, emaciated, wild creatures with plastic bottles, used wet wipes and an entire meal in food crumbs stuck to bikes and bags held together with cable ties and Sugru. But our three dramatic weeks on the trail had left us happy and content despite all the mishaps that had cost us both so dearly.

Rickie had felt a similar way about riding the Divide and so, when we talked about it together, a plan formed. Two women who move at a similar speed and who have a shared desire to communicate the physical and emotional benefits of outdoor adventures to others are a film-maker's dream. The fact that neither of us could really operate a camera and that we both have the tendency to get so caught up in riding that we might forget to film, were small facts lost in the excitement of the project. Rickie and I would ride 'together' (independently but alongside each other) with an iPhone and a GoPro between us and self-film this epic journey. What was still not clear was whether we were racing or not, and the unspoken question of whether we could do both hovered in the air.

It started the way any good adventure does: meeting strangers who would become friends. Tori Fahey (the brains behind Apidura bikepacking luggage) kindly put us in touch with her Calgary-based friends Erik, Cindy and Craig who, between them, picked us up from the airport, fed and accommodated us, then rode with us to Banff for the race start. We didn't know it then but this generosity of human spirit would be a recurring theme over the next month. Craig Stappler, a well-known name in Divide history, introduced us to Robin and Michelle who, without question, put us up in Banff the night before the race start. It was at this stage I realised just how incredible a network the Tour Divide draws around it. Robin has ridden the Divide and played host to many a nervous departee in his Banff home. The gravity of the task that faced us was obvious from the faraway look in Robin's eyes as he carefully drew out our fears and expectations over dinner the night before. Michelle's offering was more simple and practical. She solemnly removed her work badge from her Wonder Woman lanyard and placed it around my neck. This talisman would switch between Rickie and me countless times over the next twenty days and arrive in Antelope Wells covered in our blood, sweat, tears and sun cream. In time it would be given to Jenny Graham to give her strength on her round-the-world record-breaking mission and after that to a dear friend battling breast cancer. Recently it has returned to Banff with Gail Brown who stayed with Robin and Michelle before her Tour Divide attempt.

We had arrived in Banff without a clear idea of how we were going to race and film the Tour Divide. Our initial thinking was to set off the day after the mass start on an individual time trial so that we wouldn't get caught up in the race and could focus on the filming. The night before departure, we spoke to Matthew Lee, race coordinator and maestro of the Trackleaders website that allows people to follow our GPS-generated dots online. We wanted to be represented on Trackleaders so our friends, family and the primary school pupils who were matching our mileage back home could follow us, but it wasn't until we spoke to Matthew the night before that it was decided we should be included in the mass start the following morning. I think for Rickie, who tends to need a bit more time to adjust to evolving plans than I do, this news nearly blew a gasket in her mind. Suddenly, it looked like we were racing this thing. After hanging up the phone we discussed how we mustn't let the filming suffer as a result of being included in the mass start, then we took ourselves off to Robin's garage to nervously fiddle with our bikes.

That night, we watched the rain bouncing off the pavement as lightning split the sky, and I had a moment of feeling incredibly small and temporary. I move through life occasionally suffering little digs at my own mortality, but at the start of something like this your mortality squares up to you eyeball to eyeball and asks:

'You sure about this?'

My answer came easily: 'Nope.'

In the morning Banff was buzzing. Boys, bikes, bags and beards were everywhere. Robin rode with us up to the start line by the Banff International Hostel – I'd been thinking about standing astride my bike at this place for years. I was ready. I had my friend by my side. We had a joint mission. I was scared and excited and desperate to start turning my pedals in order to dispel some of my pent-up energy. This would be the last time in three weeks that something didn't hurt. I didn't think to savour that feeling then. Who does? You never appreciate what you've got until it's gone.

That first day we rode fast on fresh legs and nervous energy. We passed bikepackers of all different shapes, sizes and set-ups. There was a lot of stopping to tighten and adjust things and to take photos and footage of the intimidating snow-covered peaks we were riding beneath. We ate and changed clothing on the bike to make up time and to combat the torrential rain and fatigue that threatened, both of us digging far deeper than we had planned to this early on. A reroute due to a washed-away bridge meant a brutal hike-a-bike up and over a vertical rubble field which added half a day to the overall route, so we pushed our bikes above our heads (sliding backwards almost at the same speed) until we found ourselves among the group of riders at the head of the race. This was never our intention, but how foolish of us to think we could ride our bikes at a pace anything less than flat out. Rickie and I are bike racers and, despite our shared film-making objective, this fact is woven through our DNA.

We spent our first cold, damp night in a river valley 130 miles from the start line but were up and moving again after four hours of semi-sleep in an effort to reach Fernie for breakfast.

A word about re-emerging into civilisation after an intense bout of bike battle. Ordering food is challenging. Your brain has a time lag on it like a bad internet connection. The whole way along the route we would be asked impossible questions about the type of bread we'd like or what our cheese preferences were while we'd hop from foot to foot, squirming with incomprehension and rubbing our faces in an effort to restore basic communication ability. Empathic cafe staff would make the easy decisions for us and we would be ushered gently to one side while our order was prepared, but young or bored employees of fast food joints were more likely to stick to their script and demand all their questions receive an answer.

'Okay, ma'am, and after you've decided on your bread we're going to go right ahead and talk about all the different dressing choices we have for you today.'

Choice is stressful for me at the best of times. That's why I choose to pack two tiny bags on my bike and ride for twenty hours a day. It's hard physically but strangely stress-free because I have no decisions to make. I'm just moving forwards. Any choice is based solely on achieving that task.

Canada was wet, cold, magnificent and over too quickly. On the second day, we hauled our bikes up Galton Pass all afternoon in the rain before negotiating the snow on the summit, donning full waterproofs and clocking up our fastest speeds of the trip down to the US border. We dripped water and mud all over the immaculate floor of the border control office while bored men in uniforms laboured over our passports. I got the feeling that the day Tour Divide riders come through their office, they like to work at half-speed just to see what the effect might be on this odd group of bedraggled, wired souls. Arriving in the US felt momentous, a real landmark, and, with it, a complete change of terrain. The high, jagged peaks of Canada suddenly gave way to the vast, meandering plains and soft, rolling hills of northern Montana. We rolled along the road at 9.30 p.m. having happily left the menacing, dark rain clouds hovering over

Galton Pass and protected from them now by a barrier of vivid rainbow.

We intended to use our bivvy bags to sleep outside every night on our journey to Mexico, but after the first two days of solid rain, we got a motel room and dried ourselves out thoroughly in preparation for the following days' inevitable soaking.

After four days of riding the plains and hills of Montana we arrived in the tiny town of Ovando where the residents have wholeheartedly embraced the fact that Tour Divide riders crumple on to their grocery store porch throughout early July. The day we arrived was hot and hard going. Two hours previously I'd gone down on bended knee for something and now I had a searing pain in it. I bought a can of sweetcorn and some ibuprofen and spent twenty minutes eating and icing my knee while chatting to Whitney, the Montana-based friend who two years previously had stayed with us through Warm Showers. Whitney explained there was a storm coming in and that staying in Ovando might be wise. Sure enough the skies to the south were bubbling and darkening, and the thought of climbing up and over Huckleberry Pass wasn't filling me with joy, but it was only 8 p.m. and our rhythm of riding until 11 p.m. and rising at 3 a.m. had just been established. We said goodbye to Whitney, clambered back on our bikes and rode out into the expansive plain that led to the start of the climb. It was then that the lightning began. Big, bold claps of thunder were followed by terrifying cracks of blue light all around us and, for the first time that day, I didn't feel bothered by the pain in my knee.

The thunder, lightning and rain continued all the way across the exposed plain. This was not a good place to be in a lightning storm, but we'd made our decision and were committed now. Eventually we reached the start of the climb up Huckleberry Pass, but our relief at not having been struck by lightning while crossing the exposed plain was short-lived. The rain, and now the darkness, made descending off the pass at speed impossible. Our lights were bounced back at us by the torrential rain, meaning we had to descend really slowly, getting very cold in the process. The lights of the town of Lincoln were a long time coming that night and when we did eventually reach them we were crawling. We found another motel but were so cold, wet, hungry and tired that we couldn't even feel relief any more. The next day, having survived one final attempt at killing ourselves by setting fire to our clothing on the motel radiator, we rolled out again into the relentless rain.

There is a moment in our film *Divided* where Rickie and I are sitting on the floor of this motel room looking forlorn and shell-shocked and not at all motivated to go outside again. I was suffering obviously with knee pain and exhaustion. We both look wiped out, but I also look very swollen in my face. I would ride on for days, getting more and more swollen and sore, but knowing what I know now, I can't watch that scene without wincing.

What I didn't know then was that the maximum dose of ibuprofen that I was taking daily to help manage the pain in my knee was having another effect on my system, and in the days to come this was going to prove life-threatening.

Montana continued. Helena, Butte, Lima. Days could be ticking along relatively easily on fast doubletrack and then be slowed to a crawl by a knee-deep snowy pass or clinging mud. We changed brake pads in supermarket car parks, washed our underwear and dried it from our helmets, and ordered terrible breakfasts from cheap roadside diners. We rode uphill all morning and descended steep rocky chutes in the afternoons. We slept under the stars, in snowmobile warming huts and under trees, and occasionally we were reminded of the heart-warming support this race receives from individuals and the communities we passed through. More often than not, people were expecting us. The two leading pink dots representing female riders among all the blue ones on Trackleaders made us easy to spot on the race-tracking web page as we inched our way south.

In our urgency to complete a stretch of infamously muddy trail before the rains began again, we bypassed High Country Lodge just before the Bannack Road in southern Montana. It was 5 a.m. and although a coffee would have been most welcome, we didn't think anyone would be too pleased if we knocked on their door at this time in the morning. Thirty minutes later, a truck pulled over and Russ jumped out.

'Sorry, I set my alarm for you guys coming through, but you were up earlier than I thought. Need coffee?'

He produced a flask of coffee and some home-made cookies from High Country Lodge. We stopped to spend some time with this remarkably kind man who was keeping all sorts of strange hours to make sure Divide riders weren't left wanting on this remote stretch of desolate road. There is such kindness and camaraderie to be found on this route.

When we eventually left Montana and slipped into Idaho, it was 6 a.m. on the sixth day. We had traversed across a high plateau the previous evening and the starry sky had been so vast and bright that we hadn't needed our lights to see. We'd then dropped into the neighbouring state early the next morning, marvelling at the change in landscape and feel again. Idaho was a brief interlude, but riding through it felt like taking a deep, calming breath. Soft skies and rolling singletrack delivered us from deep wilderness to the welcome arms of an espresso hut on a busy intersection. It was here I looked in a mirror for the first time in four days. I knew I had some localised swelling in my knees, but on seeing my face I realised the swelling was not confined to my joints. This happens sometimes when I sleep outside, and my inflated stomach I assumed was the result of the gas station frozen burrito diet we had been adopting, so, although it was uncomfortable and a little inhibiting, I rode with this systemic swelling and continuing knee pain into Wyoming.

It was exciting to enter Wyoming. The Grand Teton National Park put on a fine display of needle peaks and rock formations that distracted me briefly from the growing discomfort of fluid retention. But when my knees could no longer pass my top tube without hitting it, I knew things were getting worse. My breath was now very laboured and one of my eyes was swollen almost shut. We had started moving so slowly that riders we hadn't seen since the start were overtaking us. Rickie looked over at me as we crawled up an easy tarmac gradient and exclaimed:

'Jesus, Lee, you've gone blue!'

Rickie is not known for her melodrama. A more practical, stoic person you will never meet, so when she sounds alarmed, it's time to get alarmed yourself. We stopped at Lava Mountain Lodge and had the difficult conversation I knew in my heart we were going to have to have at some point. I told her she had to go on alone. I was not about to kill myself by pushing over Union Pass that night without first getting medical help. I didn't want her to stay with me. It would have made me feel ten times worse, not least because I knew how invested in this ride she had become. Rickie Cotter is a tenacious, competitive bike rider and a fiercely loyal friend. I watched as she battled with these two parts of herself over her decision to stay or go, and in the end I made the decision for her. She had to carry on alone. We may have been making a film about this journey together, but ultimately – and this is what makes the Tour Divide so potent an experience – each of us is completely responsible for ourselves and no one else.

I watched her ride off, her face set in a grim line in an effort to compartmentalise the concern she continued to feel for me. I turned away quickly before she was out of sight and forced the lump out of my throat. I didn't feel worried, just exhausted and disappointed. I struggled with my ego as other riders came and went through the lodge, offering their condolences before speeding on into the dusk. I'd fought hard to be up in this position in the field and now all I could do was watch as it all slipped away. I booked a room at the lodge and slept a strange, numb four-hour sleep in the semi-darkness and woke to find I'd been crying. Something had shifted in me. For the first time ever I'd not been able to battle my way out of a set of unfavourable circumstances. It was day eleven. My body had simply stopped working and there was nothing I could do about it but give in.

In the morning I stashed my bike and stood by the side of the road for an hour in an effort to hitch a lift to a medical centre in Jackson, an hour's drive away. Eventually, Grant picked me up and we spent a companionable day together. He even insisted on picking me up again after my treatment and returning me to Lava Mountain Lodge, and I silently added Grant to my growing list of people to feel grateful for. The diagnosis was peripheral oedema, probably caused by a reaction to ibuprofen. I'd been taking more and more of the drug in an effort to reduce the swelling and now I realised that I'd been exacerbating the problem.

Thankfully, the swelling decreased with the help of a steroid injection from the medical centre staff and my breathing became easy again. I messaged Juliana Buhring, another endurance cyclist who had suffered similar symptoms earlier in the year, and she told me to rest more. She also explained that Billy Rice (a friend and paramedic) wasn't far behind me on the course having suffered his own medical difficulties and that Emily's brother Sam wasn't far away at Brush Mountain Lodge and could come and get me if I was stuck. This news, combined with the steroids now pumping through my system and an additional course in pill form in my pocket, gave me the strength to make the decision to carry on.

Billy and I joined forces to get up and over Union Pass at 3 a.m. the following morning. If I was going to go high again having suffered oedema it made survival sense to do so in the company of a paramedic. I'd lost a day and a half to my illness and my goal of racing the Tour Divide had slackened completely. Now all I had to do was make the most of my ride and, although I missed my friend, I realised I was really looking forward to some alone time to move at my own speed and establish my own rhythm.

It's easy to assume that riding in a pair would be an advantage on a race like this, but while Rickie and I definitely drew confidence in riding together late at night over high passes in thunderstorms, we also had to adapt to each other's pace. Rickie goes super light-weight and likes to ride up hills fast then stop to recover. I prefer to move more slowly and to keep going, and so we found that by moving together our combined moving time was slower than if we'd been on our own. I lost my rhythm by stopping in cafes; she had to temper her fast climbing efforts. I wasn't getting a chance to look around and appreciate where I was, and poor Rickie was having to adhere to my requests that we stop five times a day to set up filming shots.

With that pressure gone and my health vastly improved I felt strong and re-energised riding over Union Pass in the early hours of the morning on the twelfth day. Billy and I postholed through snow in the darkness until we emerged on the wide summit just as the sun was yawning awake and splattering the sky with colour. We descended together towards Pinedale, occasionally submerging our bikes right up to their cranks in muddy water. Then, near the foot of the descent, my bike gave a clunk and I began feeling like I was pedalling squares. My cranks were lurching about so wildly that my chainring was scraping off my frame with every pedal revolution. I got off and inspected my bottom bracket. A mashed aluminium collar revealed itself and all of the bearings had fallen out. I told Billy to go on without me.

I spent thirty-five miles grinding my chainring into my frame and moving at six miles per hour on a hot, flat road in an effort to reach the small town of Pinedale. Here, my heart sank as I realised that the bike shop was a small stand with very limited stock at the back of a general hardware store. The store manager and I problem-solved as best we could, but in the end, all that was left for me to do was retreat to the diner, drink coffee and make an alternative plan. From Pinedale, riders enter the Great Basin, a barren, sun-bleached, waterless wilderness with nothing and no one around for miles. My bike was unrideable. The closest repair shop that stocked the replacement bottom bracket I needed was 400 miles away in Steamboat Springs, Colorado. I knew this meant a scratch from the race, but I was frantically pleading with my optimistic self to salvage a solution of some kind. I didn't mind too much about the race strangely enough, I just wanted to keep moving forwards on the bike. I wanted to keep journeying and filming and sleeping out under the stars, but I was struggling to find solutions. Then Dwayne came in.

'I hear you might need a ride some place?'

Meeting Dwayne marked the end of my race, but it was far from the end of my journey.

CHAPTER 10
THE TOUR DIVIDE – PART TWO

Dwayne was a local cowboy with a day to kill. He was willing to drive me 200 miles to southern Colorado where I could reach the safe haven of Brush Mountain Lodge and the friends who had been on standby to help me when I was sick and suffering at Lava Mountain Lodge. I added Dwayne to the list of fine people I had met and accepted his offer.

It's an interesting dynamic that develops in a vehicle being driven by someone who's doing you an enormous favour. Gratitude and respect for Dwayne's altruism opened my mind to a conversation I wouldn't otherwise have had. As a Trump-voting, gun-toting, far-right, anti-Muslim Christian, Dwayne's political stance was about as far removed from my own as it is possible to get. Yet a mutual respect grew between us so strong that for the first time I felt able to really understand why someone would hold so tightly to (what felt to me like) alien values.

In 2016, the Common Cause Foundation conducted a survey that asked 1,000 UK citizens what they value. Values were gathered into two distinct groups: compassionate or intrinsic values (equality, protection of nature, social connection, health) and selfish or extrinsic values (personal success, public image, wealth). The results were staggering. Seventy-four per cent of people reported that they identified with a compassionate value set more than with selfish values. Furthermore seventy-seven per cent of people mistakenly believed that their fellow citizens lived their lives governed by selfish values. This disconnect between what people value themselves and what they believe others value is really important. It means people are less willing to engage in their communities and stand up for what they believe in because they think there's no point, and so the cycle continues and worsens and eventually becomes a self-fulfilling prophecy. But why do we think this way? One theory suggests that this is due to the message we are constantly fed by our media, our politicians, even our schools and universities, that everyone else is just out for themselves when actually the vast majority of us don't think that fame and fortune are as important as caring for each other and the planet.

Dwayne reminded me that kind, caring people can be motivated by different things and that tolerance and acceptance of difference are not only possible but can feel easy between two very different human beings. I didn't change my value system as a result of meeting Dwayne and I'm sure he didn't change his, but we both parted company with a new understanding that people who are different to us are not to be feared and that simply by being curious, rich connections can be made. Dwayne looked me square in the eye as I climbed down from his truck and said, 'You have to take self-protection seriously though, Lee. You really ought to consider getting a gun if you're going to keep riding.' Ironically, as a result of meeting Dwayne, I felt reassured by my lack of firearms. He had been my worst nightmare, the scariest thing aside from bears that I could have met, and yet here I was giving him a heartfelt high five and promising to stay in touch.

Brush Mountain Lodge sprawls on the hillside right on the Tour Divide route at the top of a gradual climb from the desert floor. Riders arrive dehydrated and occasionally traumatised, and its infamous host, Kirsten, is waiting on the wooden deck to welcome them with a hug. A hug at this point in the race can feel so good it has been known to reduce riders to tears. But before complete emotional overwhelm can set in, Kirsten has tired riders sitting down with food and drink and has already put their clothes in the wash. Most riders stop here to gather themselves and accept full hospitality, which includes comfortable accommodation, warm showers and all the food you could possibly want in a relaxed and welcoming setting. Just to add to the juxtaposition riders experience in arriving here after two weeks of ride-related torture, hummingbirds swoop and dart about, giving the place the final touches of paradise. Also waiting for me at Brush Mountain were Sam and Bernard, two friends who were supposed to be crewing for that year's Race Across America but whose rider had crashed out on the first day, leaving them all pent up with unspent energy and a vehicle full of gas, tools and bike parts, so they had detoured to Brush Mountain to offer mechanical assistance to Tour Divide racers instead. I was so glad to see them and only partly because Sam's ability to bodge a bike repair is legendary. If anyone could help me get back on the trail, it was Sam. But these things cannot be rushed. Since Grant's helpfulness back in Wyoming and now Dwayne's kindness, I was experiencing a shift in my focus and mentality. The fight was gone. Any sense of urgency had been replaced with a need to connect with people and give back to others some of the generosity I had been shown. I wanted to sit down with a beer, put my arm around Kirsten's black Labrador and watch the sunset with my friends. I could keep pushing and striving and forcing my way down the Tour Divide route, or I could pause, recalibrate and make a gentler plan. I took a long draw on a joint and kicked back on the porch to watch some hummingbirds.

A friend back home who had been watching my dot and had seen the post I had made on Twitter announcing my official scratch from the race sent me an extract from Mike Hall's blog of the Tour Divide just before he set the course record on it. Mike had been killed just three months earlier as he raced his bike across Australia, sending shockwaves through the bikepacking community and reminding us all how precious every moment we are alive is.

Mike had written:

Enjoy it, don't lose sight of just how lucky you are to be out there and, above all, manage your expectations. If we treat things as a pass or fail test we can torture ourselves over the outcome, but if we can consider it more as an experiment with an uncertain outcome from the start then we always at least get an answer.

Mike was the best.

Tempting though it was to hang out at Brush Mountain with the wonderful Kirsten for the rest of the summer, I felt ready to completely let go of any lingering performance expectations I still had and just keep enjoying this journey minute by minute. I enlisted Sam's help and he came up with an ingenious fix for my bike. Taking the bearings out of another bike's headset he fashioned a shim that then held the bodged bearing race in place and squeezed the crank arm back on. The pedals didn't exactly go round freely but they did go round and, more importantly, there was no play in the bottom bracket. If I was careful I could nurse the bike for five hours over the high mountain pass that separated Brush Mountain from Steamboat Springs where Orange Peel Bikes had a new bottom bracket waiting for me.

The next morning I rolled out again under a new flag. My dot online had changed from pink to orange, which indicates that a rider has alternated from the original route. I was no longer in the race, but it didn't matter to me. I was on my bike with my bags packed for an adventure and all the freedom and autonomy I needed to enjoy the wild places I had yet to pass through. I felt happy and content and grateful for good friends who happened to be bike mechanics.

A four-hour layover in Steamboat Springs to get my bottom bracket replaced put me almost three days behind Rickie on the trail. I felt no sense of urgency to force the repair through faster and instead I enjoyed hanging out with the friendly bunch of mechanics in the bike shop while they laboured to remove my completely collapsed bottom bracket and replace it with a new one. This was just the pace of things, and if there was no point in fighting it then I might as well enjoy it and the company of the people I was meeting along the way.

I eventually got underway just as the sun was going down over northern Colorado, leaving the heat of the day lingering in the silky night air. At midnight I bedded down on top of a pass and enjoyed the solitude of the moment. Moving solo through Colorado felt magical. It was a place I'd felt an affinity for as a young adult working for Colorado Outward Bound nearly seventeen years previously. Those thirty-day trips in the South San Juan Mountains had been extremely challenging for me as a young mountaineering instructor, but they had also offered me my first intoxicating taste of a true self-supported wilderness immersion experience. Almost two decades later I still love that feeling of moving independently carrying everything you need to survive with you. It's true freedom if you can allow yourself to really be there. This means opening yourself up to those feelings of discomfort and loneliness as well as joy. You can close everything down and feel very little while just remaining focused on the task, or you can look up and open your eyes and your heart. It's risky. You stand to lose focus and motivation, but more often than not, the opposite happens.

My knee pain continued to limit my progress until I stopped in Breckenridge and enlisted the help of Will from Howard Edge Physio. He manipulated my knotted quadricep, which he felt was the route of the problem, then k-taped my knee up for me. Together we devised a technique to help me keep on top of my seized thigh muscles. Using a full water bottle instead of a foam roller, I was instructed to lay my full body weight on the bottle and roll up and down it hourly, allowing my body weight to manage the tension out of my leg and relieve the subsequent strain on my knee. When I left his Breckenridge practice to head out into the night, he wouldn't charge me for his services. Will got added to the list.

Restored and rejuvenated by my encounters with good humans and the three-day solo time that had allowed me to slow down and breathe in my surroundings, I knew what I needed to do next. I was getting fraught WhatsApp messages from Rickie who had slipped fully into race mode in my absence and was turning herself inside out, pulling impressively long and arduous days over high mountain passes alone. In two days, she would enter the deserts of New

Mexico and I knew how much she was dreading the heat. I reminded myself of our objectives. We were making a film and completing a journey together. I had to try and catch up with her. I checked the map and emailed Matthew Lee to ensure that dropping off-route to make up time so I might rejoin Rickie was in keeping with the self-supported nature of the race. I didn't want to get in the way of Rickie's race with this film objective, but Matthew said that as long as we remained separate and independent of each other then Rickie's time would stand. I made a plan to drop down to the valley floor and time trial south on the road in an effort to intercept her before the New Mexico border. It would be a long, hot road bash avoiding three 3,000-metre passes. If I rode through the night, I'd avoid the oppressive heat of the day and make it to New Mexico before it got hot again. Riding by road was not what I had come here to do, but under the circumstances it felt right. I could claw back time and rejoin my friend in two days. I took a last mournful look in the direction of Marshall Pass, then turned south on to the tarmac.

I didn't know it then but four years later I would stand in that very spot on that roadside. Five good friends from Scotland were destined to ride the Colorado Trail Race route from Denver to Durango together one hot July and then turn around and race it back again. The exciting mountainous section I was about to swap for a two-day road ride would be enjoyed in my future. Having now ridden this gruelling, mesmerising, awe-inspiring singletrack in both directions and once under race conditions, I definitely feel as though I have scratched the itch that threatened hot tears on the side of the road that morning in 2017.

Hours after making my roadside decision, while eating Twinkies at a gas station fifty miles north of Salida, I got an email from Michael Stevens, a film-maker who lives in Gunnison, about 150 miles away from where I sat. He was interested in our film project and keen to be involved in some way. I leapt on his offer and suggested Salida as a rendezvous point. Serendipity had intervened. Michael recruited Manik, a drone pilot, and together they made their way to Salida to intercept me. I battled into a headwind that felt like an industrial-strength hairdryer but made it to Salida in time to pore over maps and make a plan. By the time Michael and Manik arrived I had worked out two options for them. They could film me time-trialling on a hot, straight road into the night in an effort to intercept Rickie on the New Mexico border, or we could travel together in their car for ninety miles back into the mountains to the town of Del Norte through which Rickie would be passing in two hours' time. To a film-maker, this choice was a no brainer. Stay up all night and get mind-numbing footage of my bum or stand the chance of filming an emotional reunion before Indiana Pass. The boys slung my bike on the roof of their car and Manik drove south while Michael filmed from the back seat. This worked for me too. I didn't want to be off-route and out of the mountains any longer than I had to be, and by travelling due west fast instead of slowly south, everyone stood to gain something.

The reunion was, indeed, emotional. Rickie arrived in Del Norte in quite a state. She was dirty and salt-encrusted, with blood from a nosebleed all over herself and her bike. A crisp packet was thrust up one nostril, but her face when she saw me in that gas station was full of joy. The boys filmed us resupplying on gas station burritos, Gatorade and protein bars, then followed us partway up the final, highest pass in Colorado before bidding us farewell. Michael and Manik had showed up at just the right time and been generous with their time and resources when we needed them most. I added them to the list.

Rickie was a shadow of herself. She'd climbed her own legs off and was now reduced to a single steady pace. We inched up the long climb together while recounting stories of our five days apart. We each got animated about the really fun bit of built singletrack that had gone on for several miles after the pass out of Breckenridge. Rickie told the story of how she had initially missed it in the dark and descended instead on a doubletrack but had been informed in the morning via social media that she had to redo it. Luckily a guy had offered her a lift back to the top to rejoin the trail where she had gone wrong. She'd lost four hours retracing her steps, but without doing so, she would have been disqualified from the race. In the back of my mind something niggled. The rules were clear about accepting lifts on the Tour Divide route. Unlike other bikepacking races, because of its remoteness you are permitted to accept a lift for medical or mechanical emergencies as long as you rejoin the route exactly where you left it. I wasn't sure a navigational error was included in this caveat, but it wasn't the time to say anything.

We had had two very different experiences while apart, but in coming back together, her broken from her gargantuan race effort and me refocused on moving at a pace that allowed me to appreciate the terrain we were passing through, we found our equilibrium quickly and re-established a comfortable rhythm up Indiana Pass. The sun sank behind the hills and the stars came out as we kept chatting and climbing, until Rickie announced she was about to topple sideways with fatigue. It had been a massive day in the hills for her, but tomorrow we would enter our fifth and final state.

New Mexico was not what either of us expected. We were prepared for vast desert plains and red dirt roads with the occasional cactus as the only source of greenery, but to begin with, New Mexico was surprisingly hilly with pine trees in abundance perched high on its rolling hills. As we travelled further south it became dryer, hotter, flatter, less populated and more economically depressed. We had to concentrate hard to ensure we had enough food and water to get us between resupply points comfortably. This is something you can only really get to grips with by riding the route yourself and we were nervous of getting it wrong so we carried more than we needed to, slowing us down but keeping things stress-free.

When we were high up we could see that for hundreds of miles the earth was flattened like a pancake and we knew that, come the final days, we would be pushing through the red desert with little or no shelter from the sun's brutal rays.

By this point our bottoms were suffering. They had been sore to start with. So much so that back in Montana Rickie had fashioned herself an extra layer of protection out of moleskin and emerged from the toilet beaming with pride at one stop and scowling with anger at the next. 'My moleskin fell down the toilet and I weed on it,' she admitted. I felt her pain. Like most aches and pains on a trip this long, the pain in our bums had gone full circle, and up until now things had been relatively pain free, but one particularly jarring, rough climb out of Abiquiu had us howling and the pain cycle started all over again. Rickie inadvertently adopted the Roman technique of hurting herself in another place in an effort to take the focus off her painful bum. She lost her front wheel going very fast down some loose trail and hit her knee hard. Now between us we had two sore knees and four sore buttocks. In fact, we would later realise, Rickie had put a hairline fracture in her kneecap, but a litre of ice cream (intended to ice her knee but which she ate instead) meant that spirits remained high. Experience had taught us that nothing, whether painful or pleasurable, stays the same.

Our four-hour sleep cycle had stretched to five as the build-up of fatigue had fully taken hold. Now, the last two hours of every evening were spent forcing ourselves to stay awake as we fought the sleep demons with conversation, songs, caffeine, sugary snacks and sometimes just grit. When the moment came to roll out our sleeping bags, blow up our mats and let our bodies sink into oblivion, it felt delicious. I'd often jolt awake a few minutes later convinced I should be on my bike and moving, then realise with giddy relief that I still had five hours of blissful sleep to sink back into, and that realisation alone made the discomfort of the entire day worthwhile. Over the last two weeks our comfort parameters had shifted in our efforts to keep riding, but what was interesting was that our range of emotions had stayed the same. This extreme way of living had simply become our new reality, and within our new boundaries, happiness and unhappiness existed to the same degree as they had in the comfort of our own homes and beds.

New Mexico was changing. We were spending longer and longer descending and it was becoming oppressively hot low down in the middle of the day. We tried to coordinate our daily stop for a sit-down meal at the hottest time of the day. It was here in a diner in the depressing town of Grants that we got the email. Matthew Lee had emailed Rickie questioning why on Trackleaders she could be seen ascending back up the Boreas Pass in northern Colorado at a speed indicative of being in a vehicle. She explained that it was because she was in a vehicle. She had rationalised, rightly or wrongly, that this would be okay as it was written in the race rules that motorised transport could be used as long as 'the rider is returned to the place they exited the course before carrying on'. But my hunch had been right. This condition does not extend to navigational errors in the Tour Divide rulebook. Rickie's dot was to turn orange alongside mine. She was out of the race. This news was too much to process over a greasy breakfast in a beige room. We got back on our bikes and rode in silence all day and into the evening. A day spent pedalling and processing had allowed the reality of the situation to come clattering in on Rickie, and by sunset, we were sitting by the side of the road while I comforted her with my conviction that this news didn't matter one bit. We both knew she had covered every inch of that trail and in a startling time under extremely unfavourable conditions, including two time-sapping course reroutes. Having her name on a leaderboard had nothing to do with that. I knew how much this ride meant to her. We all balance a little bit of our self-worth on the challenges we undertake, but when the challenge is this big, its importance, understandably, gets blown out of proportion. This was a devastating blow for Rickie, but there was never any question that we would stop before reaching the Mexican border. A quiet calm descended over us both. Now, there really was no question what this ride was about. It was all ours to enjoy and I think Rickie came to realise this over the course of the next few days with a kind of sad relief.

When Divide riders reach Pie Town in southern New Mexico, they know they are close to the end. This place is legendary for its pies but also for its welcoming community. There is a house by the side of the trail (covered in toasters, incidentally), the doors of which are permanently open to riders and hikers of the Continental Divide trail. The Toaster House has beds, a fridge full of beer and microwaveable pizza, first aid supplies, a shower, and boxes and boxes of donated trail food. We washed for the first time in more than a week and ate pizza on the deck as the sun went down. It was relatively early, but the heat had been taken out of our ride since Matthew's email and looking after ourselves felt more important than extra miles that night, so we took our five hours' sleep early in the comfort of a bed on day eighteen. As I drifted off to sleep, I conjured up an image of our absent host and silently thanked her for her generosity. Another one to add to the list.

What now lay between us and the Mexican border was 220 miles of desert wilderness. I'd been dreading this part, but as the sun rose on our penultimate day to reveal a landscape bursting with biodiversity and beauty, I gratefully conceded to myself I had been wrong in my assumptions of the desert. Sandy doubletrack snaked between trees and cacti, and in the far distance we could see with relief that what we thought would be pan flat, actually continued to undulate in and out of the shelter of vegetation.

My memories of the morning we left the Toaster House are profound. The softness of the light and the still cool air at 5 a.m. account in part for their ethereal quality, but it was more than that. It was as though the trail had smiled and held its hands up to us.

It had said: 'Well done, you two, and welcome. You're nearly there and you can't be stopped now.'

But the drama wasn't quite over yet. The Gila Wilderness is big and remote with few opportunities to resupply with food and water. We were running low on both as we made steady progress on a high plateau fifty miles from our final town. Rickie's cumulative fatigue was taking a firm grip by now, and we were reduced to singing obscure 1980s pop songs to each other and playing Name That Tune. There was also evidence of forest fires on the horizon and this made us uneasy. We'd already lost the best part of a day to a fire reroute and we didn't want to have to face the prospect again in our delicate physical and emotional state.

Some local wildfire fighters assured us we'd be fine. Yes, we'd be riding right through the fire, but it had been contained and we were in no danger. They thrust Gatorade upon us and we stayed chatting for a few moments in the shade, learning about the diversion of wildfire and examining our maps for the next resupply point. We were out of food and the only shop on our route would be closed by the time we reached it that evening. I called ahead to the tiny shop and ordered $20 worth of food to be left on their porch for us to pick up around midnight, then we rode on into the setting sun.

It was a horrible moment when we realised on closer inspection that our route didn't actually go past this stop at all and that our groceries would be left to languish a few miles up the road while we rode on getting hungrier and hungrier. We eventually arrived in Silver City, the last town on our route, having not eaten for fourteen hours and with the day heating up to be an absolute scorcher.

Two enormous vegetable omelettes, fries and a stack of pancakes made the world a rosier place, as did Erika, Silver City's premier bike mechanic at Gila Cycles. Over the purchase of an extra inner tube, Erika offered to come and pick us up from the Mexican border checkpoint at 6 a.m. the following morning and bring us back to Silver City to hang out with her and her friends. Erika quickly assumed top spot on the list, which had most recently been occupied by the firefighters of New Mexico.

Rickie and I rode on. It was 11 a.m. and we had the hottest, most barren section of dirt road still to ride in the heat of the day before hitting asphalt again and cruising the final sixty-five miles to the border. But thirty miles down the Separ Road, in forty-five-degree heat, there was an almighty bang and Rickie's rear tyre lay in two bits on the sand. The miles and the heat had been too much for it and it had shredded near the bead.

Without a word, the sewing kit was out and the tyre repaired under the beating sun until the rubber resembled Frankenstein. It wouldn't make it to Mexico, but it might just get us out of this desert before we desiccated. Rickie phoned our new friend Erika and requested a new tyre be driven 200 miles round the route to be replaced before our final road section. We'd come this close. There was no way we weren't getting to Antelope Wells now.

As Rickie nursed her tyre through the desert, moving so slowly she couldn't generate enough air flow to keep herself from boiling, I sprinted to the highway to intercept the bike shop delivery. I waited for the tyre to arrive in the shade of a motorway underpass that smelled faintly of weed and piss. Gleaming white trucks came and went, their tinted windows giving nothing away about who was behind the glass. I thought it odd that this little inconspicuous underpass had so much traffic passing through it until our tyre delivery angel explained that this close to the border, anywhere undetectable by helicopter would be a prime location for drug deal-ing. I wonder how many people's plans we ruined that day by turning that spot into a bike workshop.

I'd like to describe to you what the last sixty-five miles to the Mexican border were like, but I find I can't really. I can give you some words, but it will always remain my experience alone. My wheels went round, the air temperature dropped, the moon came up, the blanket of stars developed layer upon layer as the night wore on and the miles ticked by. These things actually happened. I know they did, but I was elsewhere. It was almost as though I'd turned my eyes inwards and was solely focused on my breath, my legs, my heart. I played out stories in my mind's eye until they became so real it was like watching TV. I was floating, flying, completely at ease and entirely alone. Rickie was somewhere nearby, but turning to look at her would have broken the spell. At that moment it was just me in this vast universe, reassessing my place in it, and with a funny, liber-ating twist of my stomach, I found I had the vague sense that I was absolutely nothing and all I'd just done was to write a tiny little part of my own history.

When we reached the border a little after midnight, twenty days and fifteen hours after we began, we kept the cameras turned off. We'd reached the end of a very personal road together, yet sepa-rately. Our mission had been to gather enough footage to make a film and to tell a story, but the award-winning film we would go on to create would always be a fiction. We could craft a story from our footage, but how others chose to interpret our efforts would be entirely up to them. Still, we knew what we'd achieved that night: two wee orange dots finally stationary in Antelope Wells. It was up to us what that meant.

My ride hadn't gone to plan, but I felt immensely proud of myself for carrying on. I could have ended my ride on countless occasions, but each time I'd made the harder but more rewarding choice to problem-solve and keep moving forward. It's so easy to let your predetermined expectations of something or of someone kill an adventure or a connection dead. The Tour Divide had taught me that I always have a choice in how I react in difficult circumstances and that by not holding on too tightly to a set outcome, something even better might happen.

CHAPTER 11
THE SILK ROAD

When life falls apart a person tends to make for the place or people that will give them the most comfort. But what if the places that give you most comfort are wild and unknown? What if you find the deepest, most profound level of comfort by exposing skin to the wind and the rain; by being made to feel the insignificance and transience of your own human existence? I often wish I wasn't that person. I'd sometimes like to seek comfort in surrounding myself with friends and family, routine and order. When I'm suffering I'd love to indulge in a routine that would help time pass and heal wounds, but that has never been the way for me.

In the summer of 2018, after a long period of trying to have children together, my fifteen-year relationship with Ferga ended. Overnight, the house we had built together became Ferga's home and not mine. Our community of friends in Inverness rallied around West Lodge and the remaining inhabitant living there, while I did what I do best and started moving.

I packed my van with some things that I didn't associate with us both too much and drove it to London where I parked it outside a friend's house and then boarded a flight to Bishkek in Kyrgyzstan. Even before I left the comfort of my friends in London, I knew I was setting myself up to experience unparalleled loneliness. My plan was to spend six weeks alone riding the 1,170-mile route set by

Nelson Trees for the Silk Road Mountain Race. I couldn't imagine wanting to race the route in June of that year, but it had always been my plan to. My circumstances had changed since I signed up to the race, but that wasn't the only reason for my ambivalence. I also wanted to have the time to experience Kyrgyzstan before barrelling through it with tunnel vision and surrounded by loads of other bike racers. The prospect of my first encounter with the landscape and people of Kyrgyzstan being in a race context filled me with shame. Kyrgyzstan is famous for its generous Islamic hospitality and I wasn't at all sure I was comfortable with the idea of a cultural exchange that might leave these hospitable people thinking Western travellers on bikes were all monosyllabic, self-centred weirdos. I was also pretty sure I would feel an affinity with the kinds of people who, for centuries, have moved their homes from place to place depending on the seasons. Nomadic tradition has always appealed to me, and in recent years the pull of an existence that embraces change has grown stronger and stronger. I had always travelled far from home for extended periods in an attempt to scratch my nomadic itch, but while doing so in the far-flung mountains of Peru or the open plains of Mongolia, I had always had our house as my anchor and Ferga as my North Star. I would come home revived and content with stories to share, and I'd feel at peace for a while at least. Riding the Silk Road race route would be the first time that I would journey solo without any emotional tether to a person or place, and I had no idea how it would go.

When things were at their worst between us, Ferga had dreamt that I was standing on a cliff edge in the semi-darkness. Out of my back had sprouted two gigantic, grotesque wings that flexed, creaked and groaned, spreading so large they obscured my entire naked frame. These magnificent, malevolent appendages of feather and muscle were so huge and powerful that their raw feral beauty frightened her even in her dream. When we separated Ferga and I still loved each other, but she felt she could no longer contend with my need for freedom.

I wasn't in a good way when I arrived in Bishkek. Right up to the end, Ferga and I were still our best selves when we travelled together by bike, and everything I saw, smelt or heard in those first unfamiliar days in Kyrgyzstan, I found myself wanting to relate to her. It took me a long time to leave Bishkek. I told myself I was adjusting to the altitude and taking my time to research the route and resupply, but the truth was, I was scared to leave the comfort of the city and the few kind souls at the Nomad Hostel whose occasional words or gestures in passing felt like my only tether to the earth. I longed for the space and the wildness waiting for me on the other side of the Kegeti Pass, and at the same time, I was terrified of where I would travel emotionally once I found myself there. Remaining in the city with a roof over my head, a Wi-Fi connection and access to good coffee was an empty kind of comfort, but there's a time and place to hang on to scraps of false well-being. Consuming to survive is not a sustainable way to live, but it's great for crisis management. In this unfamiliar place, with heart aching and no home to return to, I allowed myself to be trapped by them. Then slowly, I gently reconciled that this was what I needed right then and as I continued to push back my onward travel plans, I found little pockets of calm.

I have a vivid memory from when I was three years old, of strong arms pulling me on to my mother's smooth knee and being swaddled in a huge, warm, pink dressing gown that smelled of fusty sleep and sweet skin. Inside me, two things were happening at once. I longed to sink into her, to lie back against the full length of her warmth and familiarity and stay rocking with eyes closed in the dark, airless bedroom. But the fiercely independent wee girl I was then couldn't handle that stifling limit to her freedom. She arched her back in protest and slithered to the cold ground with a sudden desperate urgency to feel the wind on her face and experience the independence of her own limbs moving. This memory remains a painful and comforting one. Painful because that wrenching away from the warmth and comfort of an all-consuming love in order to feel independent and free to roam is a recurring theme in my life, and it felt front and centre of my suffering then in Bishkek. But comforting too, because I knew that the freedom I had created for myself was just around the corner.

I had left my partner, my home, my country and my support network. I had done the hard bit. Now I just needed to relax in warmth and comfort for a while. I needed to process my loss. I wasn't ready for the adventure just yet. That time would come, and with it, no doubt, glimpses of joy and contentment, but it wasn't for right now.

I didn't realise it then, but this marked a change in the way I would relate to myself forever. For the first time, I truly understood the precariousness of my capacity for experiencing joy.

I spent those days in Bishkek connecting with people. I went riding with a local mountain bike group. I met friends of friends of friends in cafes and began to develop an understanding of the nuanced cultural relationships that exist in Bishkek between Russians and the Kyrgyz people. I taught the eleven-year-old son of the housekeeper at the Nomad Hostel basic bike mechanics, both of us chatting away in our respective languages. I spoke to friends and family back home online and each day I wrote a journal of how I was feeling. Looking back on what I wrote now, it's possible to see when the colours started to return a little and I began noticing detail again. Two weeks in Bishkek did not fix me. It was going to take years to get over the grief of losing my old life and my best friend, but something shifted and settled. I realise now that had I bashed on over the Kegeti Pass the day I landed, the emptiness inside me would have met the emptiness of the Kyrgyz wilderness and, like a diver who hasn't taken the time to equalise the pressure in their body before going deeper, the consequences might have been disastrous.

As it was, the time I was about to spend in the Kyrgyz wilderness was still going to be very hard, but the extreme lows I was going to experience would be mitigated by the incredible highs. I believe now that the time I spent travelling solo through Kyrgyzstan accelerated my grieving process. If my grief had been a swollen ankle, it would have healed on its own with rest and time, but instead, after a brief respite, I subjected it to a rigorous, often uncomfortable heat and ice regime. I knew that by reconnecting with the natural world I would find perspective and gratitude for the life that

I had lost. I think I also knew in a place much deeper down that by suffering a little extra discomfort, I'd force a faster recovery. And so I set off from Bishkek two weeks after arriving, scared, excited, but more prepared to accept what would inevitably be a painful period of mourning.

I spent the first night in my tent just below the Kegeti Pass. With forward motion paused, dinner eaten and equipment repaired and tidied away, I could feel loneliness nibbling at the edges of my consciousness. I forced myself not to push it away and instead looked up into the starry sky. I felt a lurching panic at its vastness, but the feeling didn't overwhelm me. Instead, it reached its uncomfortable climax, then dissipated into the inky blackness leaving me feeling very, very tired. The following morning I awoke and felt as though the fever I'd been suffering from had broken. My breath came sure and steady as I continued upwards over the loose gravel mountain pass before descending all day to reach a new world of shockingly bright sandy desert.

The reason I ride bikes is because it's the best way I have found to experience flow. In his book *Flow*, Mihaly Csikszentmihalyi describes a flow state as usually occurring when a person's body or mind is stretched to its limits in a voluntary effort to accomplish something difficult and worthwhile: a state of effortless attending. Csikszentmihalyi was a behavioural psychologist who developed flow theory at the same time as B.F. Skinner was proving that humans are animals driven by reward. After years of research using rats and then dogs, Skinner proved that animals can be trained to perform arbitrary movements for tangible rewards. By giving an animal food after it performed a specific movement of a leg or a wing, he found that the animal would perform these movements again and again in order to win some food. Behaviourist theory went on to suggest that extrinsic rewards are the only thing that motivates animals to do anything at all, but Csikszentmihalyi set out to challenge this assumption. By studying artists and athletes, he believed humans were also motivated by intrinsic rewards. The rapture we feel when engaged in a flow state, whether writing, drawing or riding a bike, has nothing to do with what other people might think of you, nor does it have any connection to gaining any recognition or reward. We are constantly reminded of Skinner's theory of motivation by extrinsic reward in our consumerist society where most of us crave food we don't need, new clothes that aren't essential and other people's affirmation through social media. Less obvious is the understanding that we might achieve our most profound rewards by getting absorbed in activities that are only meaningful and rewarding to the people performing them.

For me, flow is that state you reach when everything just clicks into place and the hard thing you are doing finds its own rhythm from somewhere deep down. In these moments, discomfort, pain and fatigue still exist, but in surrendering to them I find myself moving with grace and ease and I begin experiencing gratitude for the smallest of things: a sip of water, the glimpse of a bird's wings backlit by the sun. The mistaken assumption that flow only exists in the context of extreme physical endeavour, though, is one that I held for years. The day after leaving Bishkek, as I sat on some soft grass with my back resting against a sun-warmed rock, I realised that this feeling could be cultivated in any situation and under most circumstances. Not long after that deeply comforting moment I was back to feeling lonely and focusing on reaching my destination for the day, but the glimpse of it had helped my confidence enormously.

Kyrgyzstan has it all. High alpine tundra and hot arid desert. I began each day riding upwards through the morning coolness of velvety green valleys littered with tiny white yurts, yellow smoke from the dung-fuelled stoves within billowing then dissolving altogether against the bright blue of the enormous sky. Soft green would eventually give way to sharp, shaley grey, and the dirt roads would begin to switch back and forth in improbable zigzags up near-vertical mountainsides; tyres slipping on loose rough surfaces making the scrabble for the oxygen-depleted air more desperate. Afternoons would be spent riding down through the tang of pine forests that would eventually give way to scraggly birch in rocky soil and then parched brush in cracked earth. Descending further felt like it would surely take me to the molten centre of the earth; deepening, hot red gorges narrowed the sky above to a sliver, forcing my attention to the rust orange, dusty pink and burnt red of striated sandy walls.

I was finding more and more pockets of flow now on my journey, but as I travelled further into the mountains I began suffering from the altitude and an upset stomach, which meant I was eating less and less. I reached a low point figuratively and geographically after four days' riding when I found myself on a flat valley floor. All morning I had ridden through bitter, driving rain and although the rain had now stopped, it had given way to a thick fog that was completely obscuring everything but the strip of dirt road visible just below the visor of my helmet. I climbed all afternoon on gravel road still wrapped in dense fog, but as the road surface worsened, eventually giving way to singletrack, I found I could see further ahead and I began to make out the watery edges of a weak sun. I reached the pass above Son Kul Lake and edged to the other side to prepare for my descent. I'd been so lost in my own head, with senses so starved of stimulation, that the view in my direction of travel took me completely by surprise. Below me wisps of remaining cloud stroked the vast surface of Son Kul Lake. As far as the eye could see, short, lush grass clung to every undulation in the ground making it appear more like a well-fitted carpet than anything with a life of its own. The sun which still hung shyly in the overcast sky gave off just enough energy to encourage the enormous expanse of water to sparkle where the wind caught patches of it. Semi-circles of yurts sat squat and huddled around open fires, and hundreds of horses wandered alone or cantered in small herds along the shoreline. All around me and below me was space and silence. I felt the space and silence in me rise up to meet it and for a moment felt the panic and loss again in the wild expanse of this unfamiliar terrain.

I pulled on my down jacket and hat, then sat with my back against the neatly stacked cairn of stones marking the top of the pass. I felt very alone and entirely insignificant. I sat there for a very long time grappling with those feelings and focusing on how the unfamiliarity of this situation would be charged with excitement if I was experiencing it with Ferga. As I sat there feeling very sorry for myself and being buffeted by the wind, I noticed two wild horses making their way silently along the col towards me. With every step their heads bobbed nearly to the ground then returned in line again with their strong, curved backs. Their tangled manes resembled my own wild hair and I couldn't help but project my melancholy on to their doleful faces. They stopped a hundred metres or so from where I sat. The sand-coloured one stooped to graze, but the darker horse checked itself and then continued loping towards me. I remained very still but followed it with a downcast gaze until it eventually stopped only a couple of bike-lengths from me. It dropped its noble head and snorted gently through big nostrils before fixing me with one soft, intelligent eye half obscured by a length of rogue mane. Its big, solid presence was more comforting than any human presence could have been in that moment. It would be human-centric of me to assume that that horse joined me on the col to soothe me and remind me that I was just another animal that belonged to the earth in this wild place, but that is what I felt.

I dropped down to the lake on a rare piece of singletrack, then began riding around the water's edge on yellow grass as short and even as a golf course. The weak but welcome sun had now struggled its way out of the clouds as I rode along the south side of the enormous lake. The wind from the north had picked up, whipping over the water and causing significant waves to crash against the shore, adding to the illusion that this vast inland body of water was actually the wide open sea. On the watery horizon, the sky was a brooding gun-metal grey and in the distance one end of a vivid rainbow landed behind an unusual undulation in the otherwise perfectly flat landscape. As I neared the top of a short climb, I heard the thundering of hooves and the roar of more than just a few voices. Below me, completely obscured by the landscape from the south and west, hundreds of people had gathered. The focus of their attention was a game taking place on a level piece of ground the same size as a football pitch. At either end of the pitch, two large stone cairns had been built, but from my vantage point I could see that they were hollow. In the middle of the playing field a tangle of horses and men kicked and bucked for space, sending up clouds of dust. The horses were being encouraged to turn 180 degrees on their hind legs by forceful tugs on bridles while the riders hung on by squeezing hard with their strong thigh muscles. A gap appeared in the maelstrom of riders and horses, exposing one young lad who was practically gripping on to the underside of his horse with his legs, one hand wrapped around its mane while the other tried to get hold of a black, tattered object that lay on the ground. With what looked like an enormous effort, the boy sank his fist into the object and heaved it up into the gap between his stomach and his horse's neck then, with one hand steadying his hard-won prize, he whirled around and set off at a gallop towards the cairn closest to me. The entire field gave chase with one rider beating the boy to his goal and attempting to block him from reaching it himself. The horses collided and at the same time the tattered object was propelled through the air, revealing it had four legs, a tail but no head. It spun grotesquely in the air before jarring on the lip of the stone target and toppling inside out of sight. The crowd went wild.

I had stumbled upon the National Goat Polo Championships and had arrived just in time to witness the winning goal.

I was in the middle of absolutely nowhere, hundreds of metres above sea level and looking at the most people I had seen since leaving Bishkek. I dropped down to join them and hung around for a while soaking up the atmosphere, reminded of the post-match elation I would get swallowed up in every weekend with my dad at a local rugby match. As a kid I had never really known what was going on then either, but I did like the charged atmosphere and the high-spirited camaraderie that accompanied it. It was 3 p.m. on a Saturday afternoon, and it was obvious that the vodka and testosterone had been hard at work for a few hours already. I noticed that rather than dispersing now the game was over, the men on horseback were drinking vodka from unlabelled bottles like it was water and were getting louder and less able to stay upright by the minute. It felt like time to leave.

Son Kul Lake marked another turning point in my mindset. I made a promise to myself to open up to the world and allow newness to begin healing old wounds. This meant never refusing the hospitality of the nomadic people living along the route I was riding and, as a consequence, I began spending approximately one hour in every four sitting cross-legged in yurts eating salty sheep cheese and drinking fermented horse milk, which is nicer than it sounds. I felt like I was spending more time wheeling small, smiling children around homesteads on my bike than I was riding it myself, but I reminded myself that this was the reason I had come to Kyrgyzstan in the first place. To spend time travelling through these places with respect and curiosity.

Later that evening, wet through from a freezing cold river crossing and with the sun sinking behind the intimidating glacier-strewn horizon, I heard a commotion in the otherwise desolate valley. From a yurt tucked behind a small knoll came hollers of 'Chai? Chai?' from multiple voices, young and old. Inside, the entire shepherding community was assembled, and before I could protest I was sitting at the head of the table with a glass of vodka, a bowl of fermented horse milk and the boiled head of a sheep before me. That night it wasn't just my feet that thawed out, and I found myself smiling with new memories the following day.

In the high grazing grounds of the Tian Shan mountains, three generations of the same family would sleep on mattresses on the earthen floor of their yurt. During the day, these would be rolled up neatly and stacked around the felted walls that weary travellers would be invited to lean against while taking refuge from the rain, a never-ending cup of sweet tea warming frozen fingers. Sometimes, the youngest generation could speak a few words of English, learned in the school they attended during the winter months in the valley below. I loved it when those flimsy grammar jotters emerged from battered school bags. With wide white grins, small children wearing scratchy woollen jumpers, colourful wellies and not much else would nestle beside me and the smoky dung-fuelled stove. By the light of a kerosene lamp and the sound of rain drumming on the felt roof, we would go through the alphabet together, each letter pointed at earnestly with a dirty finger followed by an expectant upward glance. The older generation of nomadic people spoke only Kyrgyz. I had tried to learn a little of this difficult language before leaving Bishkek, but every time I used one of the words I thought I had learned, I would be met with blank stares. After intense charades my meaning would be recognised and repeated back to me using a completely different pronunciation to that used at the last yurt I visited. Younger people tended to also speak Russian and, if necessary, we used my phone and Google Translate to make ourselves understood, but I always preferred the charades method of communication. The shared moment when someone has tried as hard as that to connect with someone else makes the subject of the communication irrelevant and the smile that accompanies it mean everything.

On a climb out of a small village up Shamsi Pass I was beckoned inside a small farm by a large woman wrapped in colourful layers topped by a yellow head scarf. This close to town, people live all year round in breeze block buildings with tiny windows and tin roofs surrounded by churned-up earth from their livestock's hooves. She sat me down in front of the traditional low table found in most communal spaces in Kyrgyz homes. These tables are displays of hospitality manifested in tiers of plated biscuits, dishes of home-made jam and slices of salty bread made in clay ovens on street corners or on cast-iron griddles atop wood-burning stoves. My host, like all my previous hosts, exuded warmth and kindness and kept my teacup filled to the brim as if that were her only task to complete that day. We communicated in the usual stunted way for a long time while we learned the usual things about each other's family, country and inevitably what I was doing riding through the mountains on my own without my husband and children. It was nearly lunchtime when the door to an adjoining room opened and a dishevelled man emerged in a haze of booze. He staggered slightly and pulled his trousers up over his paunch with a grunt, then left the house in his socks. There was an uncomfortable pause in our conversation as we listened to his hacking cough move across the courtyard. I looked back to my host who looked down at the table and I began to understand her delight at the possibility of passing female company. This was not an unusual sight in lowland townships in Kyrgyzstan. Kyrgyz men drink a lot of Russian vodka, and domestic violence is rife. In the townships where unemployment is high and property expensive, men usually have to travel if they want to work, leaving their families to survive. Those that stay suffer and transfer that suffering to their wives who try to keep domestic life afloat. This is in stark contrast to the seemingly idyllic nomadic existences found in the mountains where families work together to tend animals, keep house, make food and carry water. Life is hard in the mountains, but although gender differences were evident in the roles that men and women adopted, it felt like there was teamwork and mutual respect in the harsher, wilder homesteads, whereas lower down, in more built-up areas, the simplicity and order of maintaining relationships and keeping home felt more elusive. The simple satisfaction of hard graft and making do with less felt like something the bike traveller might share with the families tending the high ground. A funda-mental difference must be acknowledged between the bike traveller, who comes from a place of privilege and choice, and these families growing food to survive, but it seemed that the people I was speaking to up in the high ground, where life was much simpler, were happier and more energetic. The overwhelmed, crowded mind that craves what it doesn't have is only ever just down the valley, though.

I had ridden 870 miles in four weeks but taken the time to eat with people, watch the sky change, learn some of the language, ride graceful horses and swim in glacial meltwaters. I had moved at speeds dictated by encounters with generous people, the difficulty of the terrain and the ferocity of the weather, and as a result by the time I arrived back in Bishkek, the surface of my wounds had begun to scab over. Grieving for my old life was far from over, but I thought perhaps the vastness of these landscapes and the friendli-ness of the people of Kyrgyzstan had broken the back of my suffering.

Now friends and acquaintances from around the world were assembling in Bishkek to begin the first ever Silk Road Mountain Race. I had hoped that I would return to Bishkek ready to race, but over the past few weeks my ambivalence about racing had settled firmly in my gut (which incidentally was the only thing settled about my gut by this point). But the allure of a race goal in the company of others was irresistible, so on 13 August I rode out of the city again, but this time surrounded by a hundred other riders.

I raced hard for four days, eating very little due to my continuing stomach upset and sleeping even less, having melted my sleeping mat on my stove on the first night. I was managing to cling on to the head of the race, but my body and mind weren't functioning as I would have liked and I was beginning to entertain the notion of just stopping. It was clear that my heart wasn't in this race. I had spent a month drifting around the Tian Shan mountains, and now simply riding to get to places fast felt empty and unappealing. I was approaching a long stretch of road that would commit me to the rest of the race. I stopped at the junction and considered the ribbon of black tarmac shimmering with heat and stretching in a straight line as far as the eye could see. I needed to change the way I was feeling, and blindly bashing forward in the hope my depleted body would work my mind around to a more positive state felt hopeless. I knew what direction happiness lay in and that it couldn't be reached phys-ically. I could choose to ride north, east, south or west and it would make no difference if I didn't ride with the curiosity and calm I had begun to feel in the days before the race began.

Tash Rabat is a historic stopping place on a traveller's journey. Historians think it was somewhere traders could take stock, refuel and make further travel plans in safety and warmth. It lay six miles east in the opposite direction to the race route. I pressed down on my pedals until my tyres hit the tarmac and turned my bike in its direction.

When I went to Tash Rabat instead of continuing on the race route that day, I admitted something important to myself. My need to spread those troublesome wings Ferga had dreamt of was not something I could suppress and carry on ignoring. They were a vital part of who I was, and if I didn't spread them then the ensuing discomfort would manifest itself in other ways. Although I love racing, I had been sick and suffering as a result of it. Although I missed my former life very much, I had to acknowledge that I had been frustrated and miserable much of the time. In both cases, I had resisted, but in the end, I had had to let go and be honest with myself. Whether I had been sick from something I had ingested while in Kyrgyzstan or as a result of some emotional upheaval I couldn't tell, and, ultimately, it didn't really matter. Whether I had lazily allowed discontentedness and disconnection to dominate what was in many ways a perfect life back in Scotland or whether healthy change had been tugging at my elbow for quite some time was irrelevant. What was important was that I listened to myself now and stopped doing the things that were hurting me.

It's an interesting set of emotions that arise when you have to deviate from an expectation you set for yourself. The hollow, empty lump of failure tends to obscure whatever congratulations you deserve for the hard effort and invaluable learning you have just won. We can know this in our heads and even write eloquently about the value of trying, failing, learning and trying again, but in our mainstream social narrative, it's not okay to fail. Our politicians and business leaders know this. Being wrong is a sign of weakness. Our society rewards people who don't show signs of weakness with money and status and power, and yet I wonder what happens to our emotional state when we swallow our insecurities and put on brave face after brave face. How long until we forget what feels real?

When I awoke at Tash Rabat the next morning relief and disappointment flooded me as I remembered that my race was over. No one in the yurt encampment could tell me if it was possible to ride over the 3,964-metre Tash Rabat Pass and down the other side, but on that morning I found myself perfectly placed to find out. I set out slowly up the pass, pushing and carrying my bike then riding or running down the other side. In this unexplored little patch of mountain range, while skittering about on narrow horse track or on no track at all, I began to feel the return of happiness.

I struck out across twelve miles of pathless desert that lay between me and the original route east while storm clouds massed overhead. And this is when the magic returned. Believe me when I say that on this desolate plain there was nothing other than mud, cracked earth and tufts of stiff yellow grass. Yet on this random desert traverse in the vague direction of the gravel road that would eventually lead me back in the direction of the village of Naryn, I encountered two yurts at exactly the same time as the heavens opened. Both times I was invited in, and I sat warm and dry listening to the rain pound off the yurt felt and breathing in the comforting smell of damp wool and wood smoke. My hosts smiled toothless and wordless at me and continually topped up my cup with chai or fermented horse milk until the sun came out again.

It was in Naryn that my good friend Philippa Battye decided that the hurt-to-benefit ratio in her race was out of balance too. In fact, it seemed out of balance for approximately fifty per cent of the riders who had started the race out of Bishkek. Naryn became Scratch Village and ghostly figures made their respective ways to the end of each of their very personal journeys. For me and Phil this meant scooping up Rickie Cotter and journeying the remainder of the route our own way. We stopped for long lunches and made tea while chattering nonsense and sharing food. Moving together in good humour through a wild, beautiful place, governed by nothing but our own rules and care for each other, it felt like my emotional roller-coaster ride in Kyrgyzstan might finally be coming to a gentle stop. Three women who had started a race but had chosen to practise something different in the end dragged themselves tired but happy to a finishing party in the middle of nowhere in rural Kyrgyzstan. But this wasn't to be the final chapter to the story. The race finish coincided with the World Nomad Games, an event that takes place every two years and is as surreal as it sounds.

In a high meadow above Issyk-Kul Lake, while dead goat polo happened in a pasture above me and decorated men in fur-lined hats strutted about on fine, sleek horses, I held an eagle. Its owner gave me a thick leather glove to wear, then gently tipped the huge bird from his arm on to mine. The eagle spread her enormous wings in a brief protest revealing a surprisingly soft-looking, fluffy white torso. I moved my head reactively out of the way of the musky-smelling feathers and muscle that flailed inches from my face, but after a quick stretch of the scrawny legs and a tightening of the claws clamped to her unfamiliar perch, the bird tucked her huge wings back into place and settled. She swivelled her perfect head an easy ninety degrees to fix both bright yellow eyes on mine. As the weight of the bird and the intensity of her gaze transfixed me, my mind returned to Ferga's dream of me on that cliff edge in the semi-darkness, huge wings groaning under their own weight, and I felt the inextricable link between the eagle I was holding and the free spirit I was. This feathered embodiment of feral freedom sat motionless on my arm exuding contentedness and calm. I have no way of knowing what that beautiful, wild creature was really feeling in that moment, far from her snow-capped mountaintops, tethered to a stranger and surrounded by the noise and clatter of hundreds of people. The ethics of tethering this incredible creature to tourists for money still sits uncomfortably with me when I remember that experience, but selfishly I also remember what it was that she gave me in that moment. Perhaps unlike the eagle, I wasn't wishing I was anywhere else.

CHAPTER 12
FURRY BABIES & NEW BEGINNINGS

I always assumed that one day I would have children of my own. I imagined a strong, wilful, mischievous daughter with whom I would delightedly share the world. As the years rolled by, I began to realise the sacrifice I'd have to make to my nomadic lifestyle if I had children. Then I began wondering if I could justify children of my own at all when the world so desperately needs fewer people in it. I've never had a strong maternal urge, but Ferga always did and so despite all my misgivings and ambivalence, we tried to have children over a ten-year period. First of all, Ferga tried to get pregnant using sperm from a trusted, generous friend. We would make a monthly dash south to our friend's home where we would be handed a ramekin on a hot water bottle covered by a lace doily. It was funny and farcical but also deeply moving that someone would consider doing this for us. After a year of ramekins, doilies and syringes, Ferga still wasn't pregnant, so she began IVF at Aberdeen Hospital. In order to help us choose which sperm donor would be the best fit for us, we were given voice notes from a variety of Danish men who told us about their physical characteristics, their upbringing, their hobbies and interests, and their motivations for donating sperm to the NHS. These recordings somehow found their way on to my training tunes playlist and to this day the occasional Sven or Bjorn will still pipe

126

up to tell me how tall he is or what he likes to eat. We had a couple of promising starts on IVF, but ultimately no pregnancy held.

We discussed adoption. We had both worked for many years with families in Inverness who were constantly having their children removed by social services, and because of our level of inside knowledge, this option didn't hold much appeal. We discussed the ethical considerations of adopting children from overseas and decided we weren't prepared to add cultural and ethnic difference to our already unusual family in the Scottish Highlands. Finally, Ferga's parents offered to pay for one round of IVF with a private clinic. So in the winter before the Commonwealth Games I underwent the process of having my eggs harvested, fertilised and given back to Ferga to carry. I injected myself daily with oestrogen, which made me sore and tired and unable to train. We told the clinic how unwell I felt, but because it wasn't my body that would be used to carry the baby the clinic continued to pump me so full of drugs that I was left dangerously ill with overactive ovaries. My winter training was a washout, but much worse than that, Ferga lost our baby after carrying it for almost three months.

There is such pressure to have children. As a woman there is suspicion and judgement particularly from other women if you express ambivalence over motherhood.

'Oh, but you'll love them once you have them and you wouldn't want things any other way.'

I believed that to be true, but while I didn't have that love in my heart I was utterly free.

'They'll bring you such joy you'll wonder how you ever lived without them!'

Also possibly true, but I knew that having children of my own wasn't the only way for me to feel joy and live a fulfilled life. I was sorry that our ten years of trying hadn't resulted in us having a baby, but I was ready to move on with my life and stop living in anticipation of a child coming along. Ferga was not. Her desire to be a mother had always been much stronger than mine and so, because I loved her and I knew how great a mother she would be, after a pause to gather our strength we enrolled in the Highland Council adoption process.

It's an odd thing to hold a child who might have been your own son. Usually, a person either has children or they don't. Not many people are confronted with the children they might have had and go on to experience the painful privilege of feeling their small, soft body sit heavily against their chest. But that is what happened to me. Partway into the adoption process my relationship with Ferga fell apart and we finally agreed to separate, leaving her to adopt two wonderful kids on her own. A few years later, while I held her one-year-old son in my arms in the house we had built together years before, all the grief and disappointment from the previous years of trying and hoping and failing to have children welled up in me and I had to turn away and let hot tears spill down my cheeks and on to the soft curls tucked under my chin. Ferga put a warm hand on my back and reminded me that I could adopt children too if I wanted. But I didn't and I don't. It's complicated. It doesn't mean I don't grieve for the children I've never had. It's possible to want both things at once and want neither of them at the same time.

As a lifelong youth worker, dedicated aunt and godparent, I know that the company of children can offer unparalleled possibilities for love, fun, mutual learning, gratitude, wonder and joy. On the other hand, children can be a complete pain in the arse and severely limit the time you have to ride your bike or hold meaningful conversations with other adults. I know that by not having children of my own I miss out on feeling the unconditional love of a child, but because I don't have that love directed at me in the shape of one specific little being, I am free to think critically about the pros and cons of motherhood, and I find I have more energy to spend on the less frequent interactions I do have with children.

Being in same-sex relationships most of my life has meant that parenthood has never been likely to spring forth unplanned. Instead, I have had to consider very hard what it would mean to be a parent and be massively motivated to make it happen. If this level of consideration was a prerequisite of parenthood for us all, I wonder how many fewer children would be born each year. It seems many couples leave conception and parenthood up to chance. Many of my friends admit that this kind of non-decision-making is due to their deep ambivalence around becoming parents and that leaving the conception part to fate feels like the best way to decide the shape of the rest of their lives. Many of my friends, once top climbers or kayakers, view my unrestrained lifestyle with nostalgia and envy through a fug of snot, screaming and dirty nappies. They love their children and can't consider life without them, but they still lament their old lives and sometimes feel sad and resentful at the same time. There's no way of knowing ultimately who is happier, childless me or childful them. In fact, I'm not sure these two different ways of being can be compared. They both rely on comparisons to an alternative reality that doesn't exist. I can't ever know what I don't know and their lives are irreversibly changed due to an involuntary love for their children. It's taken me some time to make peace with that. If my partner, Alice, turns around in the future and tells me she wants to have children then my love for her will mean I'll want to reopen this can of worms, but for now, I'm content with my life. For now, I have Coire.

Coire is a working collie from the tiny island of Kerrera, which sits just off Oban on the west coast of Scotland. I was invited to Kerrera to adjudicate a kids' mountain bike event in June 2021. Oban is a four-hour drive from where I live, but Kerrera is a beautiful place with a remarkable community and I wanted to support them. I arrived off the ten-minute ferry crossing and was whisked up to the start line by my friend and race organiser, Jane. Not long after arriving, an affectionate male collie came over and leant against my legs, craning his neck to look up at me, his one blue eye and one brown eye imploring me to scratch him behind the ears. His eager, intelligent face made me melt and I found myself exclaiming that if I were to have another dog then one like this would be just perfect thanks very much. That's when Jane told me that the farm dog pressed up against my legs had just sired a litter of puppies and that she had already identified the one she would be taking home. After the kids had finished racing and all the medals had been handed out, Jane took me up to the farm to see the litter of little collies that needed homes. It wasn't a done deal. All the ambivalence I have felt around becoming a mother bubbles up when considering having a dog, too. On top of that, when my last dog, Digger (a collie–Lab rescue), died it broke my heart and I swore I would never put myself through such pain again. Yet here I was breathing in the sweet smell of puppy ears and feeling the soft, squirming warmth of their tiny bodies. I messaged Alice.

'What do you think about getting an eight-week-old collie pup from the farm on Kerrera?'

The reply came immediately.

'Wait. I'm not sure. I'd have to think about that for a while.'

Twenty minutes later Alice had sent me a series of photographs of our past adventures together with a collie photoshopped into every background.

Alice and I returned to Kerrera four weeks later to pick up Coire. Jill the farmer was running late to get the kids to school so she bundled the confused puppy into my arms and wished us luck over her shoulder as she dashed out the gate. Alice, Coire and I stood bewildered in the farmyard for a while before making our way slowly back down the long drive in the direction of the pier.

The ensuing weeks and months adjusting to taking care of this little dog were terrifying and heart-warming in equal measure. Her needle teeth destroyed all our clothes and furniture, and her constant demands for our attention left us wondering daily if we had made a terrible mistake. Yet little by little we fell in love with our furry burden and before long we couldn't remember what life was like without her.

Coire lives fully in the moment and squeezes joy out of every single situation she finds herself in. When she meets a stranger, especially a four-legged one, she wags her entire body so hard that she often finds it hard to stay on her feet. She greets everyone with the same non-judgemental, affectionate greeting. If she senses wariness or fear at first, she hits the ground and belly-crawls her way into strangers' affections, offering up her pointy wet nose to be sniffed or licked in a simple ingratiating gesture. I watch her sometimes from afar and marvel at her emotional intelligence. Her ability to read a situation and give the same amount of energy to everyone she encounters makes my heart melt. I am far more reticent when it comes to connecting with others, but watching Coire makes me feel both proud of her willingness to put herself out there to face possible rejection and ashamed of my reluctance to do the same.

It seems to me that the world would be a better place if we could all start from the same place of unconditional positive regard for others that Coire does. More often than not, she manages to set a friendly, accepting tone for making the sorts of connections from which we would all benefit more in our lives.

We've taught Coire to sit on the front of a cargo bike, balance on a bike trailer and run behind the wheels of our mountain bikes on technical terrain. She glides with an effortless grace over heather and bracken and listens to commands with a heart-wrenching willingness to please us. I cared about her from the moment I cradled her in my arms on the ferry from Kerrera to the mainland, but the love I feel for her now has somehow managed to widen my capacity to feel love for more than just her. It's as though by barging her way into my affections, Coire has managed to increase my capacity to feel love and empathy for all living things. Would I take on a pure working collie puppy again knowing what hard work and sacrifice it would mean? Probably not, but that's not the reality of my situation. We love each other now with a precious, mutually trusting connection and I wouldn't have it any other way.

My partner, Alice, is not furry. Nor is she a baby. But like Coire, my love for her has allowed me to open up to the world again in a way that felt all but lost to me after my previous relationship ended. I didn't realise it when I was single but a life based entirely on satisfying my own, self-centred desires might have been rich around the edges but it was hollow at its core. Alice and I were friends for a long time before we admitted we felt anything more for each other. The attraction had been mutual and powerful from the first moment we met at a women's cycling event in Oxford. I immediately recognised a woman whose vital energy matched my own and whose blue eyes sparkled with a humour and insight that intrigued and delighted me. We talked a lot about the terror we both felt at the possibility of losing our senses of self in a monogamous relationship, but in the end we both accepted that although it would be hard work to ensure our autonomy stayed intact if we fell into each other, the sum of us would equal more than us as individuals. I think the measure of a good relationship is if you like yourself more as a result of moving through life in partnership than you would alone. Considering someone else's needs, sometimes over my own, makes me a more patient and grounded person, but it took finding a like-minded soul to help me understand the power of that. Alice is a thinker. Her fierce curiosity and courage force me to consider what it means to remain close to another human being while staying true to myself. Her ability to hold me accountable for my thoughts and actions in relation to her means I'm not able to fall into patterns of set thinking or selfish doing. It took a lot of courage to open myself back up to being loved after my previous relationship, but in doing so it was more than just Alice's love that got in. The world was a bit grey and dull before I fell in love with her, but it wasn't until the colour returned that I realised how much I had been missing.

Our relationship is constantly evolving and deepening as a result of our investment in each other's happiness and well-being. Because I choose to love and feel love in return, I've entered into a contract with another person that insists I stay open and flexible. I feel gratitude daily for this love, but I'm not terrified of losing it. Alice and I don't hold on too tightly to each other, and we allow the space between us to shift and change as we grow together. Our shared resolve never to want to lose ourselves completely in the other person is key to this. It's our ability to perform that delicate balancing act between honouring ourselves and our partnership with lightness and humour that makes me know deep down in my bones that I've found someone I could spend the rest of my life with.

CHAPTER 13
RESOLUTION RACE

We were all out of our comfort zones on this one. As experienced solo endurance riders, Philippa Battye, Jenny Graham, my partner Alice Lemkes and I were all used to feeling in complete control of when we might eat, rest and pedal our bikes, but we had all agreed to let go of our individual riding rhythms and pair up to ride cargo bikes 600 miles in six days. While one of us rode, the other would sit on the front of the bike as cargo, each pair swapping every hour in order to manage the fatigue from the riding and the cold from the sitting. No electric assist. No vehicle support. Entirely self-supported. We would leave Edinburgh at 9 a.m. on 26 December with the intention of arriving in Copenhagen in time to celebrate New Year's Eve.

This idea began percolating after a week spent recording a podcast for the BBC World Service in Copenhagen. Three out of four journeys in the Danish capital are made by bike or on foot, and as a result, Copenhagen's air quality, noise pollution levels and the mental and physical health of its residents are noticeably better than those in any UK city. As well as making radio programmes for the BBC and running The Adventure Syndicate, I was also working two days a week as the Active Nation Commissioner for the Scottish Government. I had been tasked with helping increase levels of everyday physical activity by encouraging a system change in favour of walking, wheeling and cycling and away from car dependency, but I was experiencing first-hand how reluctant the UK is to embrace more active forms of transport. We don't like change. It's scary both psychologically and practically. This is slowly changing, but our current lack of safe cycling infrastructure in the UK is enough to deter all but the most confident cyclist. Yet the uncomfortable truth remains that transport accounts for twenty-eight per cent of all greenhouse gas emissions and of these emissions seventy-two per cent come from cars. When we consider that over half of these car journeys in Scotland are under three miles we begin to see the carbon-saving possibilities of substituting even the occasional car journey with walking, wheeling or cycling. Some people will always need to drive for work or for mobility reasons, but if we're completely honest, those of us privileged enough to drive cars make plenty of unnecessary short journeys simply because we can. When you see a city like Copenhagen in full flow at rush hour it's a beautiful thing. Bike lanes and pavements take up more space than car lanes and parking bays. Driving has become the less convenient option and, as a result, the city is quiet and calm and clean. Whatever the weather, women in high heels can be seen taking their kids to school on cargo bikes, tradespeople tow tool trailers behind them and throngs of commuters aged eight to eighty move effortlessly through the uncongested city streets on electric and non-assist bikes and scooters. Stopping at the school gates is easy. Pausing to pick something up right outside a high street shop is effortless. But it wasn't always this way. In the 1970s the people of Copenhagen decided cars were killing their city and insisted their elected members change the transport system.

When I got home, I began waxing lyrical about Copenhagen and happened to mention to my Adventure Syndicate co-director, Jenny Graham, that I had been wondering just how far it might be possible to ride one of these cargo bikes with someone sitting on the front. Deep down I knew what I was doing. Had I mentioned this idea to anyone else, Resolution Race would probably never have happened, but Jenny has always had an incredible ability to fan an adventurous flame.

The Adventure Syndicate was set up as a platform to tell the sorts of stories that might inspire more people (especially women and girls) to consider adventuring by bike, but my Active Nation Commissioner role had begun to make me realise that encouraging adventure at any cost was pretty selfish and contradictory. I was becoming increasingly aware that not everyone has the privilege of a life like mine and that the natural environment I was waxing lyrical about was having to absorb the carbon from my travel to adventurous destinations. I wasn't about to give up adventuring, but I was ready to make some changes to the way I did it so that I could continue to tell stories in authentic ways. Resolution Race became our first attempt at telling a more environmentally considerate story.

The four of us making it to Copenhagen on two bikes in one week was not going to happen if we all chose to act in our own self-interest. We were going to have to consider the collective consequences of our actions and keep our eyes on the overall objective. We discussed it and, although nervous, were all in agreement that we would sacrifice personal desires for the greater good.

Our hope was that this seemingly arbitrary and almost impossible challenge would bring the more serious global climate challenge we are all facing into sharp relief. We are all inextricably connected to one another, and the only way to make change, to achieve the seemingly impossible, is to endure some personal inconvenience and rise together with mutual care, trust, flexibility and good humour. Before tackling a daunting challenge, whether that's riding cargo bikes 600 miles or reversing climate change, it's easy to feel overwhelmed and apathetic. But the nerves and negativity we experience before we take our first steps almost always melt away as soon as we begin our actual journey and, with momentum and shared purpose, there is always joy.

Getting to the start line is the hardest part of any challenge. Weeks of preparation went into this journey and every day something would happen to make us question whether it was worth all the stress, money and uncertainty of pressing on. The Copenhagen-based cargo bike company that was going to lend us the bikes and share the expense of the project pulled out with just three months to go. Then, a month before the start of the challenge, we all decided during a Skype call that we simply could not justify flying Lael Wilcox, Janie Haynes and Rugile Kaladyte over from the US to ride the third bike and film the journey. This was very hard for everyone involved to accept, but we knew that making difficult decisions and sacrificing selfish desires was a great metaphor for the changes we were all going to have to make to tackle climate change. Instead, we recruited Oxford-based Sarah Outen and her partner, Lucy Allen, to ride an Urban Arrow; a week before we were due to set off, they were forced to pull out due to ill health.

On 19 December we were a team down and had no bikes or media crew. It felt like everything was telling us to put things on hold, but then we would remind ourselves that we didn't really have a choice. If we are to address our climate emergency we don't have time to put things off until later when the weather might be better, when our families aren't all together celebrating Christmas without us, when we'd secured some funding for the project. It felt right that we were winging it a bit and footing the bill ourselves for this one. And, as always happens when you stick to your convictions with open hearts, good luck follows.

Two cargo bike companies, Omnium and Larry vs Harry, offered us bikes to ride. MJ from the Sustrans Cargo Bike Library stepped up to receive, build and store the bikes for us. Assisting us in our efforts not to buy lots of equipment we didn't need, our good friends at Lyon Equipment loaned each bike a set of panniers. The Energy Saving Trust sourced an electric LDV van and insured it for us. Our photographer, James Robertson, rose above his job description to get his head around the logistics of driving an electric van across the continent. Jack Reed and Catherine Dunn, two students from Edinburgh University, offered to use the time for which the university's sustainability department was paying them to come and document our journey and, like James, work around the clock to drive, film and ride alongside us. Dr Kate Rawles, The Adventure Syndicate's environmental consultant and a very old friend, breathed a deep sigh of relief before asking, 'What took you so long?' Everybody rallied and helped to keep things from stalling. That's how we got to the start line at the top of the Royal Mile at 9 a.m. on 26 December 2019. The hardest part was already over.

The forecast was good. Above freezing and dry with tailwinds much of the time. Some friends and family assembled at the top of the Royal Mile to wave us off and weren't at all surprised that we weren't there until 8.59 a.m. Within The Adventure Syndicate, the theme of flying by the seat of one's pants is omnipresent.

We rolled off just after 9 a.m. with Jenny and Philippa riding one bike, myself and Alice riding the other. These pairings had taken some thought and discussion. Jenny and I have ridden together a lot over the years and instinctively trust each other when the going gets really sticky (although we are starting to realise that it might not be a coincidence that the going gets sticky when we ride together). For this challenge, however, it was decided we'd mix things up a bit. Alice and I had spent lots of time together more recently and had had the opportunity to practise riding cargo bikes as a pair in a way that Phil and Jenny had not; they had only met the year before and since then had shared more beers than they had bike rides. It was going to be a steep learning curve for them and, as we all suspected, learning about each other on the move was going to add tension to this already intense situation.

We decided as a team of four that we should remain in our pairs throughout the journey but that we'd swap bikes every twenty-four hours to keep things more balanced. The Omnium was lighter and faster but the Larry vs Harry Bullitt was more stable and comfortable, and because this challenge wasn't a race between the pairs, the constant swapping would reduce fatigue and keep all four of us moving together most efficiently. We also hoped this would send the message that this challenge was not about brand promotion.

We trundled north out of Edinburgh to intercept the Sustrans National Cycle Network that would take us 140 miles round the coast to Tynemouth and our ferry crossing that sailed for the Hook of Holland at 5 p.m. the following day. Both pairs quickly settled into a steady rhythm, taking it in turns to ride and sit in the bucket munching on mince pies and sandwiches filled with Brussels sprouts and bread sauce and croaking Christmas carols to each other. We might not have been lying on the sofa watching James Bond on Boxing Day, but there were some traditions we felt it was important to honour.

With nothing else open, we stopped for tea and to fill up our hot water bottles at McDonald's in Dunbar and had a brief conversation about whether we should include our eateries in the calculation of our carbon footprint on this trip. We were sure that McDonald's wouldn't score highly in this regard, but you have to choose your battles, or change of any sort will never happen because everyone would be paralysed by their inability to behave perfectly all the time. There's no shame in the occasional McDonald's, or in driving a car, but without an eye on the bigger picture we quickly get into trouble.

Alice had taken great trouble to work out the flattest possible route between Edinburgh and Copenhagen, but we all knew the first day was going to be brutal. There's no flat way out of Scotland except by sea and so we prepared ourselves for hopping off the bike to trot alongside it when the gradient ground us down. We'd just get comfortably wrapped in all our down clothing and inside a sleeping bag, eyes poking through a slit in the bivvy bag, when momentum would fall below four miles per hour and the passenger would be forced to jump off.

After a night in a bunkhouse in Alnwick we were all up and moving again at 5 a.m. the following morning. Our first day of eighty-four miles and almost 1,000 metres' height gain had given us a real confidence boost, but we were acutely aware that a change in wind direction or a mechanical would mean we'd miss our ferry that afternoon and the challenge would be over. Drawing on the impetus we all felt not to miss our boat meant we flew to Tynemouth mostly on safe, segregated cycling infrastructure and had enough time to test how laden cargo bikes handle in a BMX park. Not well, it turns out.

Our twelve-hour ferry crossing had everything we needed to recharge before our mammoth stomp up through Holland, Germany and Denmark, and we arrived in the Hook of Holland the following morning under a clear blue sky but with a biting wind. The sun had stained the eastern horizon a startling blood red above a wobbly grey sea, while on the shore, industrial clouds billowed out of tall cement chimneys before being swept north past wind turbines. The imagery was not lost on us.

As soon as we were out of ferry customs the route took us on to wide, fast bike paths that navigated us all the way to, and through, the city of Amsterdam. We knew we had to average 125 miles a day for the next four days if we were to achieve our target of reaching Copenhagen by the end of the decade, but at 10 a.m. on 28 December we hadn't even got going yet. There was mild anxiety hovering around both bikes and a silent resolve to keep our pace steady that morning to make up some time. No stops for coffee. Toilet breaks only at changeover time.

We left Amsterdam behind schedule, but the terrain was flat and fast, and we were now in sync with our partners. Every hour we would stop, the passenger would drop their sleeping bag and bivvy bag while the rider would put on all her discarded clothing and fill the sleeping bag with all the food and drink she'd require to recover from her hour-long effort. For Jenny and Phil this seemed to mean quite literally pouring peanut M&M's into their shared sleeping bag. The new passenger would then enjoy ten blissful minutes of comfort as her core temperature slowly dropped, while the new rider shivered uncontrollably until her core reached comfort level from pedalling. This would be our life for the next five days.

The riding through the Netherlands on that third day was really boring, but the good humour and bad singing made it more fun than any of us could have hoped for. We rode the entire length of the country on flat, well-surfaced, segregated cycle path which allowed us to focus on other important things like keeping the bikes upright. For our media team, it meant that the only way to capture any engaging footage was if they left the electric van on charge and rode out on their own bikes to meet us at changeover times or resupply points. Catherine, Jack and James would take it in turns to follow us at what must have felt like a snail's pace in the hope that we might do something entertaining. By the end of the third day, there had been plenty of slow-speed topples from stationary positions but, remarkably, no high-speed crashes. We were aching all over from these falls – not from the impact with the ground (we were too bundled up for them to hurt us much) but because everything hurt from laughing. We were just congratulating ourselves on our crash-free record when Phil rode off a newly laid cycle path into the dirt and sent Jenny flying from the platform of the Omnium. There was tense silence until Jenny wriggled free of her down cocoon to a barrage of apologies from Phil.

'I am so sorry. I'm so, so sorry. Maybe I should put my glasses on.'

We all agreed that this would be a good idea.

Dinner was called early that evening because I spilt water inside my sleeping bag and experienced a throwback to an early memory of having wet myself in my pram. Unfortunately, on getting back on our bikes after dinner, with another five hours still to ride through the dark to reach our hotel, Phil dropped Jenny again before they'd even set off. Trust was always going to be tested on this ride. We were all going to be called upon at different times to dig deep and muddle through with our partners, but that night, Jenny admitted to lying on her precarious platform wondering if she was going to survive the next three days. At the same time Phil was reflecting that while it might be okay to put herself at risk riding without her glasses on, when carrying a precious load her ability to distinguish between cycle path and mud really mattered. As we rode on that night, Phil told Jenny about her beautiful but fragile grandmother.

'She's housebound now, but I'd love to get her out. Maybe I could take her somewhere on a cargo bike!'

There was a pause as Jenny imagined how vulnerable Phil's poor grandma would be as cargo.

'From now on I'm going to ride like you're my nana, Jen! I should have been doing that all along.'

They laughed and a huge sense of relief and mutual fondness replaced the anxious mistrust of before. There were still going to be tumbles and spills, but they would never again feel like an act of carelessness.

We rode together for the rest of that night playing songs really loudly from our portable speakers, a karaoke contest on four wheels, until cold and exhaustion overtook us and we focused instead on the miles ticking down. As passengers that night, all bundled up and immobilised by our layers of down, we'd concentrate on our partner's ragged breathing, while hedgerows and stars whipped past the tiny slits we'd made for our eyes.

We thought at the start of this challenge that we wouldn't stop to sleep, but we hadn't factored in the well-being of our media team and the psychological advantage of bookmarking each day by stopping and being horizontal. Even if this was for as little as three hours all bundled into the same hotel room, we found this made a difference to how we felt about getting going the following morning.

On the fourth and fifth days, we turned away from our easterly direction and started riding due north through Germany. The wind was now fully on our backs and on one night shift together, Phil and I found ourselves riding at thirty miles per hour. Towards the end of the fifth day, we were all so exhausted that, despite the cold and discomfort, as passengers we'd easily doze off in the bucket as our partner's muscles strained under the effort of forward movement. There was something very soothing about this. As the rider, it was really disconcerting to watch as our passenger toppled steadily sideways. Remarkably, despite our deep fatigue, no one fell asleep so deeply that they fell off the moving bike, although I passed many silent minutes judging whether or not I'd be able to reach Alice before this happened.

Just outside Hamburg on the penultimate day, the Omnium's front tyre finally gave up. The sidewall was torn and the inner couldn't cope. What we didn't know was that this tyre is an extremely rare size. What we also didn't know was that the only bike shop in the whole of Germany likely to stock it was just around the corner from us. Despite having in the back of the electric van a spare Omnium that the media team were using to capture footage of us, we wanted this challenge to remain entirely self-supported and so Jenny went off to source us a replacement tyre while we sat on the street explaining to bemused passers-by what it was we were doing.

We lost two precious hours that day which squeezed us a bit for time that night. So when our replacement tyre then exploded at midnight only twelve miles from our hotel we all sat by the side of the road, addled by sleep deprivation and the cold, and gave ourselves up to apathy. It's in these moments that resolve is truly tested. We all slid off the momentum that had been carrying us forwards and allowed ourselves a moment to wallow, then silently we began improving our situation. I got my repair kit out and started sewing and booting the damaged tyre. Jenny checked the map to see how far we were from our end point and Alice called James who wasn't far ahead in the electric van. We all had a discussion on what it meant for James to return to us and swap out the Omnium's front wheel with the one the media team were carrying. In the end we all agreed that, as is the case in a more global sense, no one is going to achieve anything alone, and that by hanging on to our egos and independence we would jeopardise the entire outcome. Our team in the van hadn't helped us practically until this point, but they were as much a part of every mile clocked up as those of us turning the pedals. This was a self-supported challenge, but having a crew of supportive people in a van nearby inevitably changed the way we felt about things.

We were so grateful to have back-up that evening, but the bitter cold and our sense of independence didn't allow us to just sit around and wait to be rescued. We got the bike to a point where it was rideable without any weight on the front and took it in turns to jog alongside it in the direction from which James would return to us. Every mile the media team managed to charge the van was sacred and we had to limit the miles he drove in order to ensure the team could continue to follow us the following day. When James arrived we swapped the wheel out and got back up to speed as quickly as possible.

The morning of 31 December began like all the others: cold, dark and too soon. The electric van was beginning its final push to Copenhagen with twenty-five unplanned miles already off its clock due to our rescue the night before, and the hotel had not packed us the breakfast we'd requested. The previous night's mechanical had left us all poorly rested and grumpy with one another. Over the last

120 hours we had hardly been further than a metre apart from our partners, and that night we'd even shared our three precious horizontal hours in the same bed. There was no escape. Tiny things were starting to niggle, and despite all four of us being pretty emotionally literate and fond of each other, there was no extra time or energy to stop and clear the air. It was 6 a.m., the scheduled time for departure, but there was no sign of Phil and Jenny as Alice and I grimly readied our bike and got underway. Alice pushed off from the hotel car park tight-lipped and unsmiling with me riding backwards, cramped and uncomfortable in the bucket of the Bullitt. We had to ride eighteen miles in two hours to reach the ferry that would take us from Germany into Denmark for our last day on the road. Possible on paper but with not much room for error.

Jenny and Phil worked hard to catch us that morning and with ten miles to go, I could just make out the Omnium's front light two or three minutes behind us. We began crossing an exposed two-and-a-half-mile-long bridge in a fierce crosswind shared with high-sided vehicles, but Alice didn't falter and we made it safely to the other side.

We pulled over and waited for the others. And waited. Fifteen minutes passed and Phil and Jenny still hadn't appeared. My heart was racing despite the cold. I was panicking that the other team, who were riding the lighter but more precarious Omnium, might have been toppled by the wind into the passing traffic. I started running back over the bridge, battling images of them having been swept sideways off the bike and under the wheels of a close-passing truck. They were nowhere. I stopped and called the media team who were in a petrol station frantically trying to top up charge and worrying about missing the ferry. We were all holding valiantly to a schedule because we knew that without one we would slide off the pace and not reach our destination, but at that moment the only thing I cared about was that my friends were okay. For the first time I was really struck by how precarious a position we had all been in from the start of this ridiculous challenge and I began cursing myself for ever having come up with the idea in the first place. I continued my laboured way on foot back over the exposed bridge and then I caught sight of a tiny light far in the distance. As it got bigger and bigger I realised with a wave of relief that it was Phil and Jenny and that they were okay. At least physically. As they drew level, it was obvious that something had happened. Their faces were grim and set.

'I've lost my jacket,' said Jenny.

This didn't seem like a big deal. Between us we had enough warm clothes to make it to Copenhagen.

'It has my passport in it.'

I'm still not quite sure how we got on the ferry to Denmark that morning. We arrived at the port at 7.45 a.m., fifteen minutes before sailing, with three passports between four and no tickets. But we did. While everyone else was stopped by customs for a passport check and the media team turned back to retrace our route, hoping against all the odds that they might find Jenny's jacket and passport, we bought our tickets at the gate and rode right on to the forty-minute crossing without a second glance from any official anywhere. We all sat dazed and relieved in the ferry cafeteria drinking coffee and wondering how we were going to get Jenny home from Copenhagen without a passport. It had been a stressful morning. But now, with the air cleared again over coffee and Danish pastries (which, as Alice pointed out, in Denmark are simply called pastries), we felt nothing but mutual care and understanding for the situation we, as a team, found ourselves in. No blame, no catastrophising; this was a shared problem. Then we got a message from Jack. The one chance in a million had paid off and the jacket and passport had been found in a hedge by the side of the road. Catherine and James were on the next crossing and would chase us down on bikes. Jack would be two crossings further behind in the van, with jacket and passport, and would meet us as soon as he could. We whooped then giggled with exhaustion and relief at our outrageous good fortune.

The ferry docked in Denmark at 9 a.m. Fifteen hours remained of 2019 and we still had a relatively hilly 106 miles to ride to reach Copenhagen by midnight. We were all experienced enough to know that this was when it usually all unravelled. We agreed to stop once.

We'd shop for everything we'd need to get us to the finish line, then keep moving continuously after that.

31 December 2019 was a beautiful day in Denmark. Cold and crisp with blue skies and a fierce wind. Fortunately, the wind was forecast to swing round in our favour that afternoon and so we rode that final day with a vague disbelieving optimism that we might just pull off this crazy adventure. We made good time and by 6 p.m. we were twenty-five miles outside the city centre. Already the party was building. It's a strange fact that in Denmark the sale and setting off of fireworks is illegal except between 27 December and 1 January, so entering the Copenhagen suburbs feels like you might imagine a war zone would feel. There were fireworks in every direction, and in the built-up areas we passed through entire families lined the streets and set them off literally in our path. We paused in a petrol station to regroup and grab coffee, calculating that we'd hit the square outside the town hall at 9.30 p.m. that evening. Early? What should we do to build the drama? We weren't used to arriving early for anything. There was the brief consideration that we should stay right there in that warm garage and drink beer for a while, but then sense prevailed. We still had twenty-five miles to ride and anything could yet happen to scupper our finale. It's just as well we left when we did.

An hour later, whipping through the deserted streets, tunes blaring from speakers mounted to both bikes while dodging fireworks, Alice took a roundabout a little too fast which resulted in her hitting the kerb at fifteen miles per hour. With sixty-five kilos sitting on top of a twenty-inch wheel that kind of manoeuvre was never going to end well. Both rider and passenger sailed through the air for long enough that I had time to think to myself that the deafening bang from the front wheel was so loud it might have been a firework. Then everything hit the ground and there followed a stunned silence. I remember concerned voices and gentle hands pressing me back to the concrete, encouraging me to take a minute, to tell them what I thought might be broken. I checked myself over mentally. My hip and elbow hurt, but I could move them. I had hit the ground wrapped up like a burrito and yet through all those layers I was still somehow bleeding.

Sometimes, it's important to ponder and reflect and make informed decisions about the most sensible course of action. At other times it's best not to think too hard and just do. My hip needed a rub, Alice needed a hug, our tyre needed mending, the team needed to get to the city centre before midnight. We all sprang into action. While I got the dental floss and needle out and stitched the tyre back together as best I could, the others checked the bike over and sourced a new inner tube. Tentative jokes were cracked while Jenny placed a silent, caring hand on my shoulder. Together we repaired the mess we had made and problem-solved our way back on to the road.

We were fourteen miles from the town hall, but the Omnium could no longer travel any distance with any weight on its badly damaged front wheel. The situation was serious, but solutions were being bandied about with a certainty that never for a moment allowed us to feel that this ride might be over. We piled both panniers and the ukulele on the Omnium's platform then, tentatively, I swung a bruised hip over the saddle. Alice climbed on the pannier rack like a kid being taken to the corner shop and performed the single most impressive feat I've ever witnessed on a bike. She rode for fourteen miles on a pannier rack with only a hot water bottle as cushioning and without so much as a whimper.

And that's how we arrived into Copenhagen at 10.55 p.m. on 31 December just in time for the city's official firework display. We watched wide-eyed as Copenhagen quite literally set itself on fire, then found a tiny underground pub and had one pint each, which made us so drunk we could hardly focus on the menu in the kebab shop at 2 a.m. What we had achieved wouldn't sink in until we'd slept a bit and wandered the bike-saturated streets of Copenhagen over the ensuing days. Only then would we marvel at our own courage, which we still weren't convinced hadn't tipped over into stupidity. We'd taken a chance, one that many people had expressed so much concern over that we had begun to believe it impossible ourselves. But this ride had been a metaphor for how we might address our climate crisis from the very start. We were never sure we were going to make it to Copenhagen before midnight on 31 December 2019, but we'd squared up to the challenge and relied on our humour, compassion, mutual care and ability to problem-solve our way mile by mile to Denmark. It seemed obvious that this was the only way to tackle such a huge, overwhelming challenge. To take an enormous leap of faith then inch the rest of the way step by step. The success of this unlikely bike ride had offered us a glimpse of what might be possible by way of tackling climate change if we could just somehow manage to muster some global grit, faith and determination.

We spent the first two days of the new decade sitting on street corners sipping coffee under woollen blankets and dimmed street-lights, soaking in the muted sounds of a city where the bicycle rules and where vehicle noise and pollution are kept to a minimum. Transport is our second biggest polluting sector, but it's not surprising that the majority of us still default to cars even for short journeys when the oil industry has been so powerful for so long. Yet cities like Copenhagen prove that another way is possible, not only in achieving our carbon reduction targets but so that more of us can experience the benefits of living in places designed for people and not cars.

The humble bicycle and the spirit of the human being. Together, it transpires, we *can* perform miracles.

CHAPTER 14
REINVENTING THE WHEEL

In 2020, seventy-seven-year-old Harvie Paterson from Shotts near Glasgow discovered his deceased mother's diary from 1936. The diary described a summer holiday during which young Mary Harvie and her two sisters, Ella and Jean, rode their bikes 500 miles from Glasgow around the north-west of Scotland utilising the network of recently sprung-up youth hostels. Harvie transcribed his mother's diary and gave it to Hostelling Scotland for comment. The charity then contacted The Adventure Syndicate asking if we would consider recreating Mary's journey with a modern-day twist to celebrate our pioneering foremothers.

A not-for-profit organisation like The Adventure Syndicate is a constant struggle to keep afloat. We earn some money from film viewings, talks, events and training camps, but it's not enough to cover our running costs. Each year we tussle with the ethics of asking brands for sponsorship, but receiving money from an outdoor clothing or bike brand inevitably means encouraging more people to consume more stuff and so we find ourselves caught up in the very capitalist consumerist cycle we hate and perpetuating the myth that you need to buy stuff in order to access adventure and, therefore, be happy. So, when a charity that provides affordable, sustainable accommodation in some of Scotland's most remote and beautiful places suggests a collaboration, The Adventure Syndicate bites its hand off.

Mary Harvie was sixteen years old in 1936 and her meticulous, handwritten diary offers a matter-of-fact account of the sisters' two-week cycle tour that took them up the side of Loch Lomond to Fort William and across to Skye. The three young women returned south again via Ratagan, Fort Augustus and Pitlochry, riding up to fifty miles a day on old steel bikes with rubber tyres and rod brakes. The three sisters carried all their belongings in canvas saddlebags attached to their frames and found food and water along the way by chance. They slept almost entirely in youth hostels and it seems from Mary's journal that they took every opportunity to explore new places and meet new people along the way.

I was immediately intrigued by Mary. A sixteen-year-old girl from an old mining town on the outskirts of Glasgow deciding that riding 500 miles with her sisters is how she wants to spend her time off school during the Glasgow Fair Fortnight? Would that happen nowadays? We weren't sure. We do a lot of work encouraging and supporting teenage girls to adventure by bike, but it's not an easy sell. The girls we work with tell us that it's not because they don't want to ride bikes in the hills, it's that they don't believe this kind of adventure is for them. Yet a hidden history tells us this might not always have been the case.

Mary's journey also intrigued me historically. When Mary and her sisters rode around Scotland there were far fewer cars than there are now. There were also fewer shops, cafes and hotels, and no mobile phones, which would have made their journey much more challenging. In general, we shy away from challenge more than we need to. We are obsessed with saving ourselves time and effort but often forget to stop and ask ourselves what we plan to spend this saved time and energy on instead. Removing all the chatter of choice that we are constantly bombarded with in the twenty-first century is the reason I like to pack two small bags on to my bike and head off into the hills. It's why I feel infinitely more satisfied watching my clothes drying on a rock having washed them by hand using water from a stream than I do when I've bunged them in the washing machine at home. I acknowledge that my option to use a washing machine at all is a privileged position, and that if I had to wash all my clothes this way all the time the process might lose its appeal; nevertheless, having to perform simple, mindful tasks like this is the reason I choose to ride my bike from A to B over a period of days rather than drive there in a matter of hours. It's hard to shake free from the shackles of time efficiency, comfort and convenience when we are constantly bombarded with adverts for labour-saving devices or hedonistic experiences, but when we pause to consider what actually makes us happy deep down, we create the conditions for happiness wherever we are. Mary's journey appealed to me because it would have been challenging and satisfying in its simplicity and we wanted to recreate these conditions in our own adventure.

To do this, Alice, Philippa and I decided to create an off-road route that would roughly follow the on-road journey that Mary completed nearly ninety years previously. We'd leave Glasgow on the West Highland Way and follow it to Fort William. From there we would travel north up the Great Glen Way then cut west towards Kinloch Hourn and Glenelg before catching the little passenger ferry to Skye. On Skye we'd continue avoiding the busy A-roads by following the remote Glen Sligachan via Camasunary to reach Portree Hostel. The plan then was to return to the mainland and wiggle up and over the Torridon mountains to Gairloch before working out our return journey south again.

We toyed with the idea of using old steel bikes and wearing wool and canvas clothing as an extra nod to Mary Harvie, but in the end we decided that as this was October and we were travelling more remotely than she did, we would stick to our modern-day clothing. We would, however, ride drop-bar gravel bikes rather than using full-suspension mountain bike technology, my preferred mode of travel in the Scottish Highlands.

The three of us are massively inspired by the Rough Stuff Fellowship, a collective of hardy bike riders from the past who smilingly carried their road bikes into unlikely places, often in atrocious weather conditions. People tend to make such a song and dance of their adventures these days and post all sorts of stuff online to make themselves look like pioneering heroes, but when compared to the adventures the Rough Stuff Fellowship embarked on, these Instagram posts appear false and empty. We forget that this stuff is not new. Our grandmothers have been doing it for years and with far less advanced equipment than we have at our disposal. Technological advances are a wonderful thing, but we do tend to default to innovating our way out of difficulty or discomfort when sometimes it's simply not necessary. Why reinvent the wheel?

In our efforts to capture the joy that keeping things as simple as possible often brings, we planned to limit our reliance on modern mapping software and bike technology to align our trip with the level of complexity Mary might have experienced. Alice, Phil and I live in a world where we are constantly being encouraged to buy more stuff, have different experiences, or practise more mindfulness in order to feel good. All three of us work hard to cultivate minds that rest easy in the knowledge that we have just enough exactly as we are so that we can subvert this clawing, unattainable consumerism. Gratitude for what we do have then becomes a subversive act. We stick two fingers up at the adverts and the food binges, and we turn away from the constant longing for something more. But it's easier said than done!

We would have our friend, photographer and film-maker Maciek riding with us because our job was to gather enough footage to make a short film and to tell our story on social media, selling not stuff but the concept of travelling sustainably between hostels. But from past experience we knew that posting to social media daily while on an adventure resulted in staring into our phones all evening rather than playing Twister in the hostel lounges and enjoying each other's company. Mary's diary was a factual account written on paper in pencil. We got the feeling from reading it that it was her own aide-memoire rather than for anyone else's entertainment and that she was far more concerned with her current moment than documenting her adventure. Although it's often the job of The

Adventure Syndicate and we love telling stories, we all hate the pressure of feeling we have to sidestep our current realities to speak to a virtual audience, so we agreed that we would focus on the journey and each other and post to social media once the trip was over.

I felt hugely motivated to do a good job in promoting the fantastic hostelling network and its philosophy. Youth hostels helped democratise access to the great outdoors when they first appeared in the early twentieth century in Germany. Scotland followed suit in the 1930s, offering affordable, shared accommodation on the edge of its finest outdoor environments. Swathes of people from industrial Glasgow would travel north to make use of the youth hostels and breathe the clean air of the countryside, and they continue to do this today. Cycling did for women what hostels did for the working classes. Mobility justice, especially for women, was realised when the common bicycle became popular among the working classes. For the first time many people were able to travel autonomously and for free, and as far as I'm concerned cycle touring (whether camping or staying in affordable, sustainable accommodation) still epitomises freedom, happiness, simplicity and social justice.

These days, as in those days, we hear a lot of anger about the litter and noise that new demographics of visitors from built-up areas sometimes bring to our lochs and glens, but I find it incomprehensible that we choose to focus on this rather than on the unfair allocation of natural green space in our built-up areas for children to play in. Surely the fact that some people suffer poor air quality and noise pollution inside their actual homes due to other people's dependence on motorised transport is more worthy of this level of anger. It seems to me that reducing levels of litter and noise in our wild places is a matter of education and a willingness to share our sense of guardianship over nature with people new to the outdoors and that demonising them and excluding them from nature further exacerbates the problem. It's too easy to be blinded by disrespect from a few unthinking people who behave selfishly and not see the catastrophic losses our natural environment suffers from in the name of economic growth and innovation. For all of these reasons, project

'What Would Mary Do?' became a multi-faceted piece of adventuring and storytelling. What began as a request to create a short film and social media campaign about the history of hostels turned into an opportunity to tell the story of female emancipation, mobility justice and nature connection. We do like to shoe-horn in the important stuff.

Philippa, Alice and I currently form the adventuring element of The Adventure Syndicate (though we often draft in other like-minded, hardy souls such as Jenny Graham). The three of us work well together both on- and off-road and on and off bikes. Our friendship has been consolidated by countless mountainous missions where the carrying aspect of the route has definitely outweighed the riding element. There are a handful of people in the world I would trust to accompany me into these unpredictable environments. Ferga Perry, Rickie Cotter, Durita Holm and Sarah Outen are some of the others that fit that bill, but it's not their physical ability that gives me confidence in them. It's their willingness to reach for their sense of humour, compassion and resilience when the shit hits the fan. If the weather turns, we lose the trail or we find ourselves wading through bog, having the confidence that your teammates aren't going to get angry or sad but will instead start chuckling and then problem-solving is extremely important. The worst thing that happens when Alice and Phil have had enough of a situation I have inevitably put us in is that they go quiet. Their pace will not slow and they will not complain, but they exude grim determination as they make their way through bog or over hill.

At the start of this trip, Maciek was an unknown entity. He and his wife Monika had been official photographers on GBDURO the previous year, a self-supported bikepacking stage race from Land's End to John o'Groats. We knew he could take great pictures, fly a drone, make short films and ride a bike, but we didn't know whether he could do all of these things at the same time. We needn't have worried.

It's important to us that the photographers or film-makers we work with travel alongside us on our adventures. Having a vehicle pop up at road junctions and a film crew leap out to document a journey that they are not part of feels disingenuous. Finding competent bike riders and talented storytellers like James Robertson, Catherine Dunn and Maciek Tomiczek has meant The Adventure Syndicate can craft stories while being part of the adventure itself, which makes a far more authentic and engaging end result. It puts a lot of pressure on them, though. We have to ride long distances, navigate, eat and usually camp. They have to do all of that and handle a camera too. On a particularly memorable bike ride from Bristol to the French Pyrenees, Jenny Tough, Jenny Graham, Rickie Cotter and I got the ferry timings wrong and had to team time trial to make our crossing. Carrying cameras and multiple lenses, poor James tucked in behind us and hung on for dear life while we collectively reached speeds of up to thirty miles per hour. He turned green and then ashen, and we had to calculate how much time we'd lose by stopping to make him drink a can of Coke versus taking it in turns to push him up hills. Humanity prevailed and we did stop for a few minutes. Luckily James, like all our long-suffering creatives, responds very well to sugar. It's a question we ask at interview. We made the boat with minutes to spare, and James spent the crossing going into cramp and reflecting on his life choices.

———

Left Glasgow at 7 a.m. on 14 June 1936 up Old Edinburgh Road and Anniesland Cross ... we had tea at Luss then spent two hours sunbathing in Ardlui ... we stopped to explore the Falls of Falloch ... before arriving at the newly built Crianlarich Hostel at 6 p.m.

MARY HARVIE – DIARY ENTRY

On 18 October 2021, on the other hand, the weather was terrible. The conditions were lining themselves up nicely for this to be a challenging week with just enough variables to keep the outcome unknown – the definition of adventure as far as I'm concerned.

There's a two-mile section of the West Highland Way near the northern end of Loch Lomond that is an absolute horror story as far as cycling is concerned. This boulder field within a forest has the loch squeezing you from one side and the steepness of the hillside from the other, and walking it is hard, let alone getting a bike through it. Every time I find myself there, muscling my bike over rocks and through gaps in the trees, I make a mental note never to attempt it again. But time distorts memory in a remarkable way, and I find myself there again and again. This time I was determined to learn from my past mistakes. There is a line that can be drawn between diving into a satisfying challenge and making an annoying mistake. It's one thing to go into the unknown and deal with adverse conditions as they arise. It's another to know what's coming and put yourself through hell anyway. It's a step too far to then also take your friends. Alice had quite sensibly vetoed the idea of carrying pack rafts to get us round this section of shoreside trail, so we made an alternative plan to catch the tourist boat that pauses at the isolated Inversnaid Hotel and be transported across the loch to the busy road on the west side for a few easy miles. As we made our way north along the eastern edge of the loch we watched the huge white-topped waves pitch and roll over the surface of the angry water. The trees were offering us some respite from the howling wind, but their tops were bending alarmingly above our heads and the rain was falling from the sky with the same urgency that we were feeling to catch that boat. Some incredible boat handling went on to allow the Inversnaid boat to dock long enough in the massive swell to bundle four cold, wet cyclists and their loaded bikes on to it. We drank hot chocolate with rum in it as we pitched and heaved across Loch Lomond to Tarbet then joined the busy A82 north towards Crianlarich.

Later we looked at pictures from the 1930s of what is now the A82 looked like then: a serene, peaceful, barely surfaced road meandering up the side of the loch. Mary, Ella and Jean must have had a lovely time pedalling north along it. By contrast, Phil, Alice, Maciek and I flinched from the close-passing cars and lorries as we grimly trucked north, stopping briefly at the Drovers Inn for a pint to steady our nerves and dry off a little.

As soon as we could we rejoined the West Highland Way and

paused at the Falls of Falloch just like Mary did. Sticking to our off-road alternative to the busy roads was never going to be a faster or easier way to reach our accommodation each night, but what was the urgency? I've been guilty of ditching a set route to join a busy road just to make up some miles many times. When the weather is bad or light is fading sometimes it can be the safest thing to do, but often, in my experience, taking the easy road when it isn't necessary doesn't always leave me feeling that fulfilled. At the Falls of Falloch we stopped to ask ourselves how it was we wanted to behave on this trip. If our adventure was to truly embody Mary's then we wouldn't be reaching for our phones to get weather forecasts, research faster routes or find out where the next pub might be. We'd be remaining in the discomfort and excitement of not knowing. We'd be staying in the moment and appreciating the weather and the terrain, however uncomfortable or sublime it might be. We wondered how much more uncomfortable the two miles of hike-a-bike on the other side of the loch might have been compared to the busy A82 and agreed that it wouldn't have been more or less uncomfortable, it would simply have been different. So before leaving the falls we set our intentions again for this trip. We wanted to 'Be More Mary'. This became our mantra for our remaining days' riding. Whenever we found ourselves tempted to reach for the information so readily available on our phones, or divert to the road to just get to where we were going a little faster, we'd ask ourselves, 'Why? What for? What would Mary do?'

In the 1930s there was less choice and convenience, and it felt to us that there might be a richness there that we could tap into, so we all agreed we wanted that more than reaching our destination faster each day. Clichéd as it sounds, we wanted our journey to *be* our destination.

Left Crianlarich and headed for Black Mount. Here a lorry stopped and offered us a lift to Ballachulish and we didn't refuse. Each holding our own bike, we sat on the lorry. Then we crossed over the ferry and up to Fort William to stay at the Glen Nevis Hostel.

It seems even in the 1930s racing ahead when the opportunity presented itself was a real temptation. But while Mary raced ahead to Glen Nevis, we resumed our meandering journey north on Sustrans route 78 which takes cyclists over to Ardnamurchan on the Corran Ferry before returning them to Fort William on a tiny passenger boat run by the Highland Council mostly so that kids can access school. Mary then reported riding towards Mallaig:

> ... *on mostly excellent roads until Glenfinnan where the road becomes dreadful! Stones, holes and no road at all in places and so we jumped into a lorry for 5 miles to get beyond the worst of it while motorists had to turn back towards Fort William.*

To travel along this road to Mallaig now would render Mary's description from the 1930s incomprehensible. Buses, lorries and tourist traffic make this an uncomfortable road to ride even in October, so we joined the Caledonia Way instead to make our way north on canal paths and drove roads until we eventually reached Ratagan Youth Hostel, but only well after it got dark.

We considered the differences in our experiences as we rode north. Since the 1940s our transport infrastructure has been designed in favour of motorised transport. We've designed out pavements and green space and replaced them with dual carriageways and parking bays. We didn't think through the health, environmental and social impact this might have, but if you try to ride your bike to Mallaig along the otherwise spectacular A830 it comes clattering home to you just what we have done to our wild places. Even more worryingly, stand on the pavement of any rat run in any city centre in the UK at 8.40 a.m. and consider how impossible it would be for the children living on that street to walk or cycle to school. The priority we give to the people who can afford motorised transport suggests we have lost sight of the important things in our society such as health, equality and our environment. It feels like we have traded happiness and connection in favour of speed and efficiency. And for what? To earn us more money? To be more productive?

We wondered what Mary would have made of our modern-day priorities.

The next day, Mary, Ella and Jean crossed on the ferry to Armadale and began their ride up through Skye. The roads here were reportedly rough enough to give them multiple punctures, but they reported:

> … riding 30 miles over moors with nothing to see but sheep and heather. Skye was a lovely island then, very peaceful with wild birds on the shores and pheasants in the heather.

We crossed to Skye via the timeless turntable passenger ferry at Glenelg rather than by the popular Skye Bridge, then cycled to Broadford before making our way into the heart of the Cuillin Mountains.

Before Mary was even born, the traditional township of Camasunary Bay on Skye was cleared to make way for sheep grazing. Nowadays it sits desolate and dramatic against a backdrop of sea, sky and black, foreboding basalt. Phil, Alice, Maciek and I dropped into Camasunary Bay on rough doubletrack at that magical time of day in late autumn when the afternoon light is becoming too fanciful to be taken seriously. We sat in front of the now down-at-heel bothy looking out across the sea loch to the south and marvelled at our luck. To be here, on this planet, at this time, with these people, in this light, with our health and privilege and perspective felt unbelievably fortunate.

Maciek eventually made us get up and stop navel-gazing so he could capture some images of us riding through dramatic Glen Sligachan in the fast-fading daylight. With the calls of the rutting stags reverberating off the steep-sided glen and the gloomy cloud descending to obscure the tops of the mesmerising Black Cuillin, we made our way north towards Sligachan and, eventually, Portree Hostel. This moment in the semi-darkness with the primeval sound of bellowing deer and the oppressive, cloud-shrouded Cuillin Mountains on either side of us was to be the high point of our trip. Our luck would soon run out.

Meanwhile, back in 1936, after a couple of days spent riding more rough roads, sleeping in hostels in Dunvegan and Uig, more sunbathing and swimming in the sea, Mary, Ella and Jean rode back to Kyle of Lochalsh to catch the tiny passenger ferry that's since been replaced by the Skye Bridge. In 1936 they met no one for miles along what is now the A87, the road where we chose to pile our bikes on to a Citylink bus because we knew how treacherous sharing it with motorised transport could be.

Our paths crossed at Ratagan one last time before Mary and sisters began making their way back south by Fort Augustus, Pitlochry and Perth. Mary Harvie reports riding in more sunshine, stopping to explore castles, take tea in someone's house, eat bread and cheese as there was nothing else, and riding long miles on rough surfaces being helped by the occasional motorist.

But we couldn't follow Mary south. Sometimes, things don't work out as planned. We got off the bus at the Skye Bridge and made our way to Coulags in Torridon to begin our most technically challenging day in the mountains yet. Coulags to Annat is a classic mountain bike route that I'm very familiar with having ridden it countless times. It was perhaps the confidence I felt that was my downfall. While descending a bit too fast towards Annat in torrential weather and on a fully laden drop-bar bike, I went over the bars and landed hard on my head and shoulder. I've crashed my bike enough times to know when I've really hurt myself and when I've got away with it. There's a split second on impact when you're left wondering which of those categories your current situation falls into before either grief or relief floods your system. This crash was bad.

In my racing days a crash like this would have been my worst nightmare. It would have meant weeks, maybe months, of frustrating, painful rehabilitation and a premature end to my hard-fought season. In 2010 I took a fairly insignificant jump during a race at Dalby Forest in Yorkshire but landed my bike badly. I bounced violently over the handlebars and landed flat on my back with sickening force. I lay on a spinal board in Scarborough Hospital for four hours wondering just how bad my situation was. Eventually the X-rays came back and revealed to me and my horrified sister (who was fortunately with me at the time) the extent of the damage. My bones have never broken easily, but in this case it might have been better if they had. The impact had forced my collar bone and top two ribs out the front of my sternum. There was nothing hospital doctors could do about such an injury. They told me to rest and take pain relief until the torn ligaments and muscles around my chest had healed. They speculated that physiotherapy might help relocate my bones, but they couldn't say. They also weren't sure how this would affect my strength and mobility in the future. It could have been so much worse, but in that moment it felt like my life was over. In a split second my body had morphed from being in peak physical condition to a complete wreck. I spent a further six hours lying flat in the back of my sister's van as she drove me home, moaning at every bump in the road, tears of self-pity and pain pouring down the sides of my face. I then spent the rest of the summer sitting one-handed on a static bike in my porch watching the Tour de France until depression consumed me and Ferga and Kim bundled me back into the van once more for a walking trip in the French Alps.

It was on this restorative, gentle trip in the autumnal Alps with my partner and sister that I realised that there might be a subconscious pattern to the illness and injury I suffered. Dislocating major bones had not been a deliberate move in my race at Dalby Forest, but there was no denying that for the past few years, when I reached peak pressure in my racing calendar, I would get ill or injured and be forced to hit pause. I would feel intensely disappointed at the time but, if I searched my soul, there was another emotion woven through the disappointment, and it took me until this injury and my subsequent rehabilitation to realise that the underlying emotion was relief. Racing was fun, life-affirming and rewarding, but it was also stressful, relentless and exhausting. My coaches didn't realise I felt this way, nor did my male team members. The following year British Cycling's performance coach, Phil Dixon, explained to me that some women's finite testosterone levels mean they will often run out of drive to race partway through a season. While my male colleagues could replace their spent testosterone more easily and show up ready to fight every weekend between March and September,

I realised that my ambivalent feelings around racing might be (on some level at least) hormonal. My subconscious was showing a wisdom I didn't have, or possibly wouldn't admit to having, by physically removing me from the pressures of the race calendar. Illness or injury still happens occasionally today when I try to cram too much into an already busy schedule, but it happens less often and is far less dramatic when it does. I'm a slow, stubborn learner, but I do learn eventually.

On this day, two miles above Annat and the road through Glen Torridon, I used my split second to scan my neck, head and shoulder before I passed out from the pain. I came round in the group shelter with Phil on the phone to mountain rescue and Alice gently saying my name over and over again. In the time I had been unconscious Alice had taken control of the situation, got us all in the group shelter and watched in horror as my lips turned more blue and my complexion more ashen. She was visibly relieved when my eyes flickered open and I insisted that Phil hang up the phone immediately. The pain in my shoulder was intense, but I knew my head and neck were intact. As a member of Braemar Mountain Rescue Team, the thought of being rescued off a hillside and the subsequent teasing that would ensue filled me with actual horror. Instead I gathered myself and instructed my team on what I needed to get off the hillside and along the road to Torridon Youth Hostel. One half of the management team of the hostel is also Torridon Mountain Rescue Team's first responder. If I hadn't got myself off the hill and to her door, Emily would have been sent out to triage my situation. Instead, she filled me full of pain relief and together we hatched a plan to get me to Raigmore Hospital in Inverness. I didn't feel the underlying relief I might have felt in my younger days, which made me fairly sure this hadn't been a subconscious intervention to slow me down. I had just been a bit reckless and unlucky. But there is always a silver lining to any situation and this time the silver lining arrived in the shape of Jenny Graham. I called Jenny and told her I had fallen off my bike on the Annat descent and that I needed her help to get back to Inverness. She said she would be there in an hour.

X-rays this time thankfully revealed only a torn AC joint which Jenny and I felt was best dealt with using Prosecco and single malt whisky. It wasn't the ending we had planned to our Mary Harvie project, but in many ways it was a better one. Phil, Alice and Maciek joined Jenny and me at her home in Inverness where we consolidated our friendship further with a karaoke microphone and more Prosecco. We were pretty sure it was what Mary would have done too in the situation.

In a post-Prosecco fug I considered the learning to be found in Mary Harvie's journey with her sisters and whether it might offer some insight into how to lead healthier, happier lives today. Bathed in the clarity that often follows a painful accident and subsequent celebration of life, I considered what might happen if we continue to focus on a growth economy rather than prioritise our health and that of the planet. All the data shows that our continued growth economy model will exacerbate inequalities and accelerate climate change and yet, in my experience, new technology and more stuff doesn't bring me anything near the same contentment and happiness as sharing simple experiences with the people I love. If we choose not to reinvent the wheel, might we realise that less is actually more?

To test this theory, two years later we met Mary's seventy-nine-year-old son, Harvie, at Port Charlotte Youth Hostel on Islay. We were on another promotional trip for Hostelling Scotland where we had been tasked with visiting the ten whisky distilleries on the island by bike and making a short film about it. We were tight for time and stressed about the content we had to gather and the online story we had to tell, but when we met Harvie, all of this just fell away. The Port Charlotte Youth Hostel guardians, Karl and Lorna, are two of the kindest, gentlest souls imaginable. The culture they craft in their hostel of care and consideration for fellow hostel users in turn encourages everyone to take the time to connect with one another and the environment that surrounds them. It was to Karl and Lorna that Harvie first gave his mother's journals in 2020, and so it was to them we owed our gratitude for the success of project 'What Would Mary Do?'.

We spent the day with Harvie riding slowly around the island, sitting in small cafes and visiting the local heritage museum. That night we ate together at the pub and shared stories and ideas at a slower, more considered pace than the three of us had grown used to. Our interaction with Harvie had the same rich quality as I enjoy with my mum, who is a similar age to him. It can be hard to still my busy mind and ignore my to-do list in order to tune in to her, but as soon as I do, I realise it's me who has the most to gain from the connection. Lesley has an annoying but remarkably astute habit of offering pearls of wisdom as I leave her home. It's often something along the lines of 'slow down' or 'make space' (although once on my way out into the rain for a training ride it was 'can I not just give you lift?', which wasn't as intuitive and wise as her other pearls). She's right of course about the slowing down and the making space. Doing so allows chance and creativity the opportunity to flood in. Our time spent with Harvie in Karl and Lorna's hostel on Islay reinforced this. As did a chance occurrence just as we were leaving. A partially sighted couple from France turned up on their tandem. They were also roughly following Mary Harvie's route having watched the film *What Would Mary Do?* on Hostelling Scotland's YouTube channel and were startled to find the three of us and Harvie at the hostel where it had all begun with Karl and Lorna's curiosity and care.

It seems, try as we might to get away from the fast-paced, screen-based world of short film production and social media, these are the very vehicles that generate more connections and other people's stories of adventure. We would have to find a balance between old methods and new if we were going to keep the richness of slow personal connection with each other and the natural world and still touch people across the world with our fast, en masse, online communication.

There must also be time to unplug completely. Not everything needs to be documented. I'm not sure that taking time out of my busy schedule to race long-distance, self-supported bikepacking routes is what my mum meant by 'slow down'. I'm sure as she leans anxiously out of her doorway to plop this particular pearl in my path she has in her mind appreciating an art gallery or sitting and listening to the birds. These are rich experiences indeed, but sometimes I feel a physical need to draw myself out to the very limits of my ability and there is one race in particular that has the capacity to do this.

CHAPTER 15

THE HIGHLAND TRAIL 550

The Highland Trail is a 550-mile self-supported mountain bike time trial through some of the most remote and rugged landscapes in the Scottish Highlands. Approximately fifty people begin riding a set route on a certain day every May with the ambition of riding, pushing and carrying their bikes 550 miles from Tyndrum to the North-West Highlands and back. Only commercial services available to the public can be used to resupply from or to rest in. Riders choose how and when they eat and sleep, but the clock never stops. The entry fee is a recommended donation to the John Muir Trust. There are no prizes and no support. It's a race like no other.

I wake up under a cold damp fog somewhere below the Orrin Reservoir. It's 4 a.m. and daylight is just beginning to nudge at the horizon. I tried to get to Contin last night, but the concentration required to squint into the billowing fog at high speed was too much for my tired brain. Instead, I pulled off this doubletrack at 1 a.m. and have slept well in this den of bracken next to a small stream. I am glad I stopped when I did. I shiver uncontrollably while I clamber clumsily from my sleeping bag and with shaking hands I pack up my bike. I throw one leaden leg over my bike and ease myself back on to the saddle then start pedalling slowly down the glen. I ride for two hours before the sun takes control of the damp morning air and transforms the still hanging fog into delicate wisps of cloud suspended just inches above the ground. A herd of deer stand alert on a grassy hillside as I ride close by. It looks like they are standing on clouds while all around them the dew on the grass dances and sparkles in the sleepy sun. I am close enough to be able to watch their ears twitch, but they are hovering shadows to me behind the thin fog. I feel extraordinarily lucky to be here.

JOURNAL EXTRACT, 2019

I've had countless conversations with people who insist that those of us who choose to ride something like the Highland Trail 550 do so because we are sadomasochistic, because we have attention deficit disorder or because we are insecure and have something to prove. While all of that might be true to a greater or lesser degree, I believe we all choose to challenge ourselves on rides such as the Highland Trail for a variety of complex and interwoven reasons. To assume that our end goal is to experience suffering misses the point entirely.

The state I'm seeking when I set out on a mission of endurance is not pain and discomfort. It's the opposite. Of course I experience uncomfortable feelings in the course of a 550-mile non-stop mountain bike race, but I do so in my day-to-day life too. Pretending the hard things don't exist and attempting to avoid them is what causes us so much suffering. Endurance for me doesn't mean gritting my teeth and shoving my feelings away so I can keep going. It means feeling resistance to pain and discomfort and allowing it to flow through me. By being in a situation where I have no choice but to make friends with it I gain perspective, strength and gratitude. It's why, ever since I was very little, I've felt this insistent tug outside and towards the unknown.

I'm looking at a large, imposing mountain in the Fisherfield range near Dundonnell but upside down and framed by my own legs. It's really hot. I've taken off my helmet, placed my swollen hands on two perfectly placed rocks either side of the stream and lowered the top of my head into a puddle of clear, cold calm. The water comes up (down?) to my eyebrows and sends a delicious chill through my whole body. Perfectly framed by my mud-

brown, bloodied calves and the lower parts of my black shorts is the classi-
cally shaped mountain of Beinn a' Chlaidheimh. The greens, greys and reds
of the hill shimmer in the heat against the solid, bold blue of a perfect cloud-
less sky. I smile. Or am I frowning? This is weird.

I was very lucky growing up. I had enough warm and generous adults around me with adventurous sparks of their own to ensure mine was never extinguished. I had access to green space and the trust of my parents and community to explore it alone. Children need boundaries, but clipping their wings entirely has serious implications for them as adults. I often wonder who I might have become had I not had the space and autonomy to play outside my house, ride my bike or walk the long way home from school.

I am an adult who survived the wing-clipping and yet I still allow the heaviness of routine and obligation to deaden my curiosity and sense of adventure more than is necessary. Finding balance is hard and the only way I have found to do so is by hitting stop occasionally. I appreciate it sounds counterintuitive, but the all-consuming challenge that is racing self-supported through the Scottish Highlands *is* me hitting stop. I've tried for years to sit still and meditate. I can't. I'm like the excited kid at the back of the class who wants to explore and discover rather than be told or taught. I understand those kids. We need motion to think and to find calm. It takes special energy and extra compassion to deal with us, but we're worth it. We have some great ideas and lots of energy to implement them. Having worked with these kids for years, I agree that it's much easier just to squash them back into their seats and dampen their disruptive spark. But easy all the time becomes boring very fast.

It's day two and I've been riding since 3 a.m. The sun is now setting behind
Suilven as I pick my way through some rough, rocky singletrack on a
coastal headland near Lochinver. The moon has just popped up and is
casting a blue-grey glow on the sea below me. I am tired and hungry but
massively moved at the spectacle before me. I stop my bike and watch the

moonlight turn the water into a silvery dance, delighting in every twitch
and minute change in colour and contrast.

I have also had conversations with many people who insist that it
is disrespectful to move with your head down on a bike through
wild places and that it can't be possible to appreciate your natural
surroundings when moving through them at such a pace. But I don't
think it's possible to move through difficult, remote terrain smoothly
and with ease without first stopping to doff your cap in admiration
and awe. Omit this humble gesture and a wild place remains intimidating. Someone who attacks a trail with anger or frustration will
slip, slide, curse and stumble their way along the Highland Trail and
will probably find themselves questioning their life choices and
feeling utterly exhausted. I know this because I can also be that bike
rider. But when I have the head space to remind myself that slow is
smooth and smooth is fast, the world falls back into place for me. It's
easy to become trapped in the belief that you must be going as fast
as possible all the time, avoiding anything or anyone who might
distract you from your self-imposed goal. I am as guilty as anyone of
behaving this way in a race and in my daily life, but the folly of this
becomes more apparent in these wild, special places. Here I am
compelled to stop, breathe and be. After I have taken that moment,
my balance on the bike is better, I'm more alert, I can manage
discomfort more easily and I notice that my breath is less forced.

I'm high above the causeway in Fisherfield. This is without doubt my
favourite place in the entire world. When I reach it at 4.15 p.m. on day
three of racing, I think I must be in second place. But as Fionn Loch comes
into view 300 vertical metres below me, and the drama of the Letterewe
range stands facing me on the other side of the glen, I stop, lay down my
bike and sit still for ten minutes. I listen to absolutely nothing other than
the vague charging of water somewhere far below me, and struggle to make
sense of the beauty that exists here all the time, day and night, whether I
am there to witness it or not. This is not typical bike racer behaviour, but
could it be that overall it actually makes me faster?

I find that riding long distances through remote wilderness while snatching only smatterings of sleep will, ultimately, render me defenceless and wide open to the vibrancy of the real world. This level of physical output grinds me right down until I'm as vulnerable and susceptible to joy and misery as a child. It's then that my senses become open to the heart-stopping wonder and fragility of our natural world. This wonder is right there all the time, it's just that it's easy to let the colours dull when you're busy and distracted all the time.

It's definitely night-time now, but I don't put on any lights yet. The moon is huge and bright and the air is still warm and I don't want to break the spell. I can still see just enough to travel at speed on the predictable fire road that will eventually lead me south towards Coire Lair, but as I pass a large expanse of moon-blue grass, two wild white horses rise luminescent out of the gloom. They toss their manes and contort their bodies into a wild, interwoven dance, cantering about playfully and casting sideways glances at their incredulous human audience. I'll be the first to admit it's been a long day, and that's the reason I find myself performing a double-take, just to make sure they aren't sporting unicorn horns from their long noses.

I've remained awake and moved through countless sunsets, sunrises and fickle weather systems and felt very scared and lonely. I've suffered countless crises of confidence in the cold, wet darkness before the sun comes up or the rain stops. I've moved through these dark, uncomfortable places and emerged utterly stripped down physically and emotionally. What follows is a period of intense calm and a humbled, energised conviction that I am both utterly insignificant and a vital part of something much bigger.

I like who I become on these long bike rides. In focusing on one big physical challenge in the mountains I can harness a flow of natural energy. I stop feeling stressed about everything by being consumed by the stress of one thing, and I deal with negative thoughts in the moment rather than allowing them to fester in my subconscious. In this set of circumstances, something as hard as racing 550 miles becomes easier than navigating my everyday life.

A cold, high, remote mountain plateau is a scary and uncomfortable place to imagine yourself being in the middle of the night, but when that is your reality, there is no room for anxious imaginings. Until you are standing there you won't know if you'll experience a calm, steady focus, a gripping dread or a wild euphoria, but whatever happens, these are some of the best conditions I've ever found to fan creativity, connection and gratitude into a full-on flaming ball of fire. By allowing myself absolute heart and soul freedom while I move self-supported through wild places on something like the Highland Trail, I realise that happiness is right there under my nose all the time.

I've stopped to eat a chocolate bar in the shade of a tall boulder. An inquisitive insect has started helping itself to the melted chocolate on the wrapper, naively unaware of the danger it's in. I'm watching its mouth and front legs working on its lucky find and, although it is in my way and slowing me down, I feel instinctively that I don't want to hurry it. Eventually, I carefully smear a tiny piece of melted chocolate on the boulder behind me and place the startled little creature on top of it. By taking my time in that moment I feel like I've really squeezed every last drop out of being alive and connected to what is happening around me. By drinking in all that detail, I feel full and replete. I have also just had chocolate which tends to make even the worst of circumstances better.

My Highland Trail might be someone else's new job, separation from a long-term partner or the welcoming of a child. Flinging ourselves headlong into a new adventure with an unknown outcome is a terrifying prospect, but in not doing so possibilities remain things of fiction and to me it's always felt wasteful to be scared of something that only exists in our imagination.

I used to think there was a time and a place to practise self-care and empathy but that the middle of a bike race wasn't it. Now I wonder if the circumstances that produce the highest levels of stress in us might be some of the best places to practise these ways of being. I've come to the conclusion that treating myself like a small child who I care about very much helps me manage the stress that would otherwise have me thrashing about in frustration. When my nephew was four he didn't know when he was hungry. The discomfort he felt, which usually manifested in shoe-throwing or foot-stamping, made the prospect of eating anything unappealing in the extreme. But as a caring, objective adult I would gently but firmly insist he eat something. My body needed about 8,000 calories in a twenty-four-hour period to keep moving forwards on the Highland Trail, but the thought of food made me feel physically ill, especially towards the end of the ride. There is a lot of trust involved in swallowing another grim flapjack when my child-like brain is screaming that she feels sick and wants to be left alone to throw her shoes around. But pausing to take care of myself has always worked, and I feel instantly better and a little embarrassed by my naive, belligerent four-year-old self. I still catch myself in my everyday life yelling, 'Oh for f**k's sake, Lee, COME ON!' In those moments, I'm as frustrated with myself as I was with my nephew when he wouldn't leave his Lego set and get his shoes on – but I would never have shouted at him like that. I'd have used humour, bribes, patience and compromise to get the desired outcome. So why would I think that by shouting obscenities at my own tired, hungry, four-year-old self I'd get a good outcome?

I'm only forty miles from the end of this ride, but my four-year-old self is freaking out. She needs more than a handful of Jelly Babies right now. She needs a full-on, swaddling cuddle followed by a warm bath. This is when it all counts. I sit a moment longer at the foot of Buachaille Etive Mòr and try to talk her down. I promise her sleep and food and warmth in just a few short hours' time. I promise that, if she will only trust me enough to meet me halfway, I'll take care of her when the sun comes up. She puts her wee hand in mine and reluctantly we get back on the bike to finish this journey.

The attributes commonly associated with sporting prowess are akin to those found in successful business people and many of our political leaders. Strength, power, confidence, goal focus, charisma. As children, our definitions of success, and our road map on how to achieve it, are very straightforward. Winning is good. Losing is bad.

Being rich is good. Being poor is bad. Being strong and capable is good and the opposite of that is to reveal our vulnerability and expose our failures. This is bad. Dangerous even. All human attributes have a shadow, but historically we've colluded with each other to shine a light on some and not on others.

I'm finding it hard to tear myself away from the weirdly prehistoric beauty of this relatively unvisited hillside above Loch Maree. I have to stop and drink this place in. There's a natural infinity pool on the edge of a wide grassy bowl about two-thirds of the way along the Postman's Path; a piece of nearly imperceptible singletrack that meanders through bluebells and ferns for eight miles to Letterewe Lodge. The heat has left the sun, but I feel sticky with salt so I drop off the path to the pool and plonk myself fully clothed in its smooth, black waters. The cold water whips away two days of dirt, salt and dried blood, and when I eventually stand up I feel like a baptism of some sort might have just taken place. Over my right shoulder is an angry setting sun and over my left a shy, pale moon. In the space between I stand dripping wet, feeling wildly alive and replaying my massive day of riding in my mind's eye. I woke up below Suilven near Lochinver at 3.30 a.m. and I've ridden, pushed and carried through the bright light and harsh heat of an eighteen-hour day. The distance I've covered feels difficult to comprehend.

The bizarre dichotomy of placing myself on a start line in order to practise compassion, patience and gratitude is not immediately understandable. Traditional sports coaches would probably laugh out loud, but what if we were given the time and space to explore other ways to win and, further to that, consider what winning or success actually looks like? Could a shift away from our growth economy mindset that supports extractivism and social inequality to a well-being economy, designed to serve people and planet, make more of us healthier and happier?

We are hardwired to move faster in the face of adversity in order to escape it, but the faster the world goes the more important to me the pause between thinking and acting becomes. Perhaps by practising this pause I might find that not only do I become happier but I might also perform better. Maybe in letting go of what I think I know I might discover there are other ways to win?

It's the day after completing the Highland Trail 550 and I feel like I have just awoken from a dream – a four-day adventure of moving through the most elaborate of film sets, the most magical of dream worlds. In riding this trail that stretches the length of the Scottish Highlands, I have flown with the birds who called to me each morning and bounded with the deer who then stood watching me quizzically from hilltops. I've been changed by this. Unquestionably, mind-alteringly changed. To live like this. To move like this. To manage my body and mind like this has taught me more about myself in four days than an entire career of elite racing ever did. And the thing is, it was easy. Not the pushing of the pedals or the carrying of the fully loaded bike over col after col or the three hours of sleep a night or the managing of my food and equipment. Of course that felt hard. What was easy was the simplicity of the doing and being. Despite the discomfort, tiredness and hunger, the miles slipped effortlessly away. Hours disappeared in the changing of the light. At no point did I feel bored or distracted or desperate to be somewhere else in the way I often feel in my normal life. Because when the ride just becomes life and your only objective is to keep moving forwards through it, then things become very simple. Nothing hurts. Not really. The painful points come and go like the weather and in the end, like the weather, are neither good nor bad. Today I can't walk, but of course I can. The midges are unbearable, but of course they're not. I'm exhausted and I MUST sleep, but I can stay awake if I have to. I'm very hungry, but a few more moments of feeling this way won't kill me. Everything feels possible and every feeling is a privilege. Nothing feels impossible, boring or unsatisfying unless I choose it to. This was just a big bike ride, but I find that as a result of riding 550 miles in four days, I am quite changed.

Lee Craigie completed the 2019 Highland Trail in three days and twenty-two hours, making her the fastest female to ever complete the route and one of only a few to finish in under four days.